CHANCERY LANE / ERNESTO BEDMAR ARCHITECTS

MASTERPIECE
SERIES

CHANCERY LANE / ERNESTO BEDMAR ARCHITECTS

INTRODUCTION BY **BYRON HAWES** | EPILOGUE BY **MAX STRANG**
PHOTOGRAPHY BY **CLAUDIO MANZONI & ALBERT LIM**

OSCAR RIERA OJEDA
PUBLISHERS

CONTENTS

INTRODUCTION   010
BY BYRON HAWES

DESIGN   014
DESCRIPTION   016
SKETCHES   020
PRESENTATION DRAWINGS   028

CONSTRUCTION   040
WORKING DRAWINGS   042
PROCESS   068

THE BUILDING   096

EPILOGUE   178
BY MAX STRANG

APPENDIX   180
BIOGRAPHY   182
PROJECT CREDITS   184
PHOTOGRAPHY CAPTIONS   186
BOOK CREDITS   200

INTRODUCTION
BY BYRON HAWES

'Architecture should speak of its time and place, but yearn for timelessness.' – Frank Gehry

Just minutes from Singapore's famous Orchard Road shopping district, Chancery Lane occupies a place of privilege and tranquility in the city's nature-filled inner sanctum.

Singapore is atypical in both its density and its plethora of wildlife. A relatively tiny peninsula nation of roughly 275sq/m (720sq/km), boasting a tropical climate, and natural rainforests and wetlands, it is essentially a city-state that somehow pairs a hyper-dense urban environment (all of its 5.5 million residents live in the city proper) with extensive flora and fauna.

The nation's culture is comprised of myriad merged groups; particularly straits Chinese, native Malay and Indonesians, and Indians, and her arts, cuisine, and design histories reflect that.

The city's architecture is similarly diverse, running the gamut from traditional shophouses to utterly modern high-rises to traditional colonial black and white houses which, despite their central location, boast vibrant gardens full of monkeys, monitor lizards, and the occasional cobra the length of a Range Rover.

'God is in the details.' – Mies van der Rohe

Ernesto Bedmar was born and raised in Córdoba, Argentina. After studying architecture there, under the legendary Argentinian architect Miguel Angel Roca (who himself studied in the country under the tutelage of the immortal Louis Kahn), he practiced architecture in far-reaching places from South Africa to Hong Kong, eventually settling in Singapore, and domiciling there for the past three decades. He is justly recognized as not only one of the country's most fêted contemporary architects, but also as one of its most representative.

His work has taken him throughout the region, completing projects in Malaysia, Indonesia, Bangladesh, India, Bali, and more. And while Bali isn't a country like the rest of those, there is a particular architectural style inherent to the island, which has been hugely influential to tropical modernist architects, perhaps best espoused by the late, great Geoffrey Bawa.

Bedmar's cross-border, cross-cultural architectural work and design are heavily informed by his unique interpretation of modernist tropical styles. Like Singapore herself, his work is steeped in a host of cultures, traditions, and aesthetics.

In our 2019 book, 'In The Tropics', a two volume monograph of three decades of Bedmar's work, I wrote: *'[his] output, is in no uncertain terms the positing of a new paradigm in the evolution of tropical architecture. A veritable manifesto for a certain style of living, that synthesizes the indoor/outdoor dynamism at the heart of the tropical experience; ecologically forward before it became 'en vogue,' locavoracious before the term existed. In short, a new modality within the language of modern architecture, conflating, rather than juxtaposing, the conveniences of contemporary residential living and the experiential nature of the tropical climate and environment.'*

Geoffrey London, in his essay on Bedmar in the 2007 book 'Romancing the Tropics', discusses a 1978 project Bedmar worked on with Roca; a three-storey housing complex in Soweto, a township on the outskirts of Johannesburg, South Africa. The architects were surprised to find out that no one wanted to live on the top two floors. It was, as London writes, 'an early exposure to the lesson of the local'.

'Recognizing the need is the primary condition for design.' – Charles Eames

Tropical residential architecture
Bedmar's works, while wholly modern, speak to a rich history of SE Asian influences. And, yet, they feel somehow beyond both time and

BYRON HAWES is a New York-based writer and designer. He is the founder of the underground design magazine *The Après Garde*, and a co-founder of I-V, a boutique architecture and design firm whose projects include a recording studio for OVOsound, Campari's Canadian HQ, and Spin Toronto. He is contributing editor for architecture and design at *Hypebeast*, and previously served as a consulting editor at *Architectural Digest China*, as well as contributing to publications including *Monocle*, *Wallpaper*, *Apartamento*, and *Azure*, amongst others. He has also authored or co-authored the books 'We Are Wonderful: 25 Years of Design and Fashion in Limburg', 'The Landscape Architecture of Paul Sangha', 'Bedmar & Shi: In The Tropics', 'Post-Industrial Brutalism and the Daiquiri', and several titles in ORO's Masterpiece Series.

place. While the centralized courtyard and natural materials inherent to Balinese architecture are a primary feature of the Chancery Lane House's design, one gets the distinct sense that this house would be equally comfortable on the Côte d'Azur or along Quintana Roo, though perhaps not quite as geographically appropriate.

Perhaps one of the reasons for this sense of geo-agnostic quotidian tranquility is the fact that, despite the property's staunchly urban setting it feels removed from the hustle and bustle of one of the world's most vibrant cities. An oasis in the midst of a storm, if you will.

By placing structures on three sides surrounding the central courtyard/swimming pool area, and by creating walls (and then camouflaging them with flora), the entire property feels almost like a setting unto itself; neither urban nor rural; neither ingrained nor removed.

Tropical residential architecture is a broad category. One that fuses a host of styles, concepts, cultures, and material palettes. A sense of peace is to be inferred, but also a sense of place. Materiality and geo-spatiality coalescing in the pursuit of subtle sublimity.

Bedmar says: 'Growing up in the countryside, or in close contact with it, was the reason why materials that filled my collective memories — such as stone, adobe, or straw — have become important elements of my current architectural language', and this carries forth in his realized output.

An aesthetic language writ from texture, light, shadow, and form in the same manner a poet parses syllables. Iambic architecture.

Climatic awareness

A tropical climate is defined as a non-arid region where the average monthly temperature never falls below 18 degrees Celsius (64 Fahrenheit), while remaining frost-free and consistent in temperature throughout the year.

Singapore, as with much of SE Asia, has high temperatures year round, as well as a powerful solar radiation, high humidity, and abundant rainfall.

A central tenet of tropical residential architecture is the seamless transition between indoor and outdoor spaces; with both forming a sort of symbiotic whole. And while some icons of the discipline, Palm Springs Midcentury Modern, for example, exist in dry desert environs, others, such as Chancery Lane, must be designed to handle monsoon seasons and precipitous rainfall.

Chancery Lane protects its inhabitants with shielding structures on all sides; clever shading of various outdoor areas (such as the overhangs shielding the barbecue area from sun or rain) and closable slatted shutters on the inward facing bedrooms and master suite.

Conclusion

Tropical modernism is an expression of fidelity to a place; a culture, aesthetic and ethos.

It is a statement of understanding and appreciation. Of living within an environment rather than reconfiguring an environment to suit one's needs.

I'm sure it is easy to forget all of the small details that go into making this house what it is. The calm amidst the surrounding chaos. The aesthetic and environmental cues. The purpose driven lifestyle it allows.

However, even if one does, there is simply no way to overlook the fact that, with Chancery Lane and Ernesto Bedmar, one is viewing one of the genre's most beautiful residences; a creation by one of the discipline's true masters.

DESIGN

DESCRIPTION

The Chancery Lane house is a perfect representation of Bedmar's ongoing interaction with the new language of tropical residential architecture. Evocative of the simple, open structures of times past yet possessed of a modernity of spirit perfectly in keeping with contemporary life, the house conflates, rather than juxtaposes, indoor and outdoor spaces in perfect harmony.

Entering the property involves passing a stacked stone fence thematically reminiscent of the 'angkul-angkul' fences that surround traditional Balinese properties, which are used as much to isolate views of the property as to protect inhabitants. Once inside, the building is laid out in a 'U' formation, with the house oriented around a central courtyard comprised of a large rectangular swimming pool floored with dramatic polished blue and black stone, and a sheltered outdoor bbq and living space. A pair of structures made into a single one, delineated through separations between the west and northern cross-sections via floating bridges on the second floor.

Visitors can enter directly into the outdoor spaces, highlighting the courtyard, while the pool is flanked by a landscaped lawn and a wooden deck. The pool extends past the perimeter of the 'outdoor living space' with a single wooden bridge across the elongated body of water linking the terrace with the bbq area. A dramatic black spiral staircase leads from the outdoor living space into the main house above, the second floor fitness facilities hang over the exterior space, providing shelter from tropical storms, as a slatted blonde wood installation wall allows sunlight onto the bbq area while also providing shade and protection.

On the northern side of the ground floor, living and family rooms look directly over the garden and swimming pool, and are designed as a single large space, delineated by a central partition wall. Both interior and exterior structural walls of these spaces are glass, the exterior looking out over a reflecting pool and lush garden of trees and fronds, creating an air of space and tranquility. To the west, a central dining room features a spacious polished-wood table for 12 and a dramatic line of pendant lighting. Wooden slatted shades create an air of privacy from the garden outside when drawn, allowing a spatial sense of the exterior spaces even as the space retains a sense of intimacy. The kitchen is adjacent, and maid's quarters are just beyond, contributing to the ordered flow of the property.

A main staircase of recess-lit blonde wood separates the living and dining spaces, and leads above to a library/study and guest bedrooms on the western side, with a small bridge connecting to the northern 'pavilion' containing the master quarters. A spacious bedroom is walled in a fabric of flecked grey and muted woods and leads through to a tile-walled master bath containing an oversized soaking tub and rainshower. Wide-slatted wooden flooring and modernist ceiling fans continue the overall feeling of muted elegance and calm. Past the bathroom lies the master dressing room and closets.

The roof pitches gently upward to the east, allowing for windows along the top of the interior walls of the western building, imbuing the space with natural light but protecting it from direct sunlight.

All spaces are directed inwards, utilizing the central courtyard as a natural focal point, underscoring the dramatic symbiosis between indoor and outdoor space.

SKETCHES

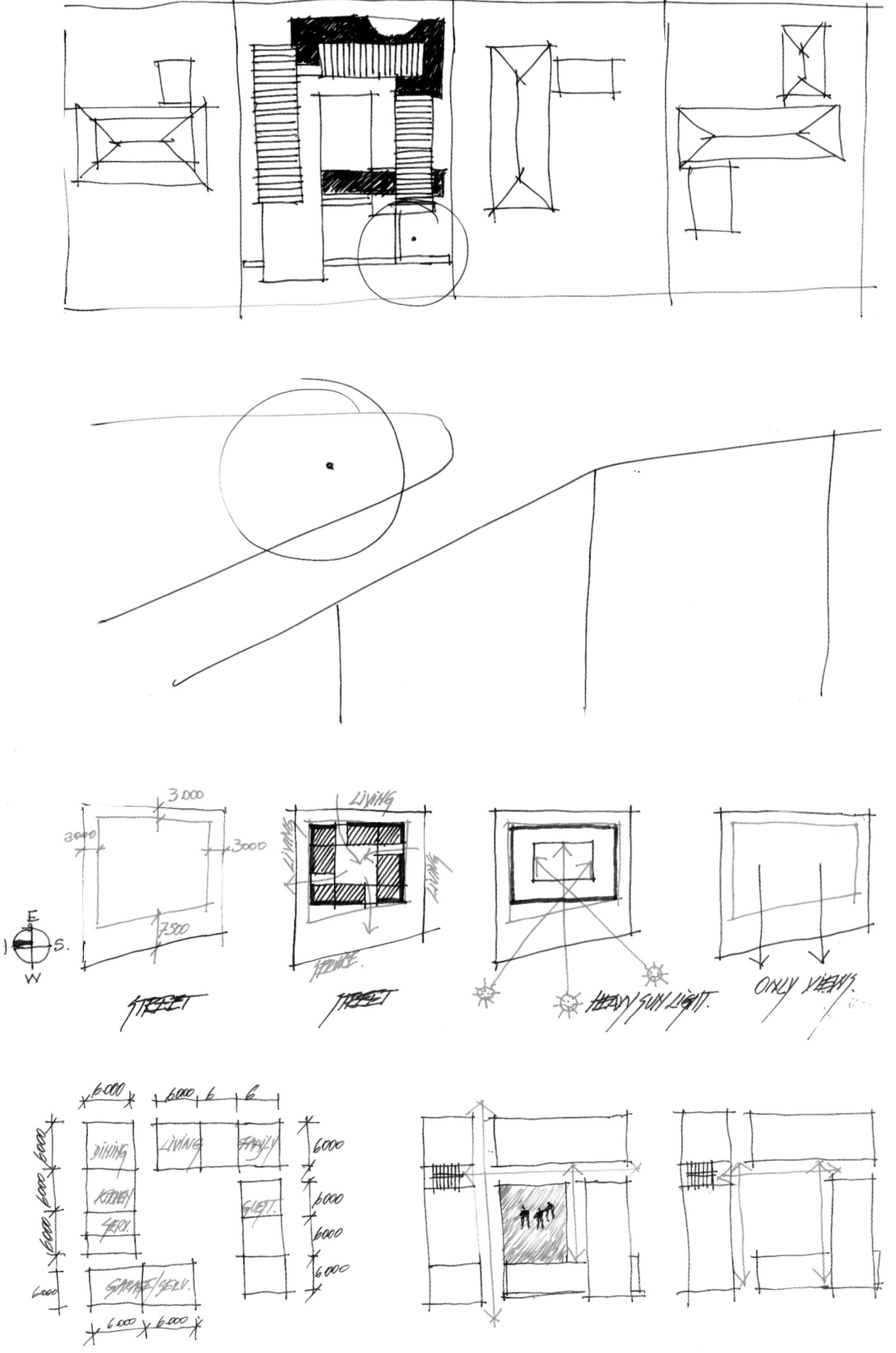

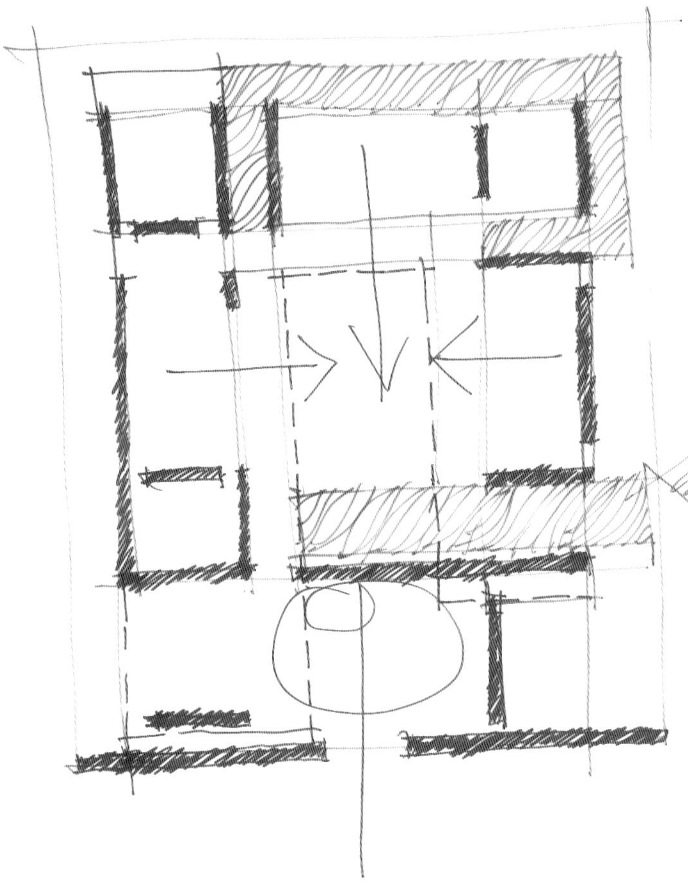

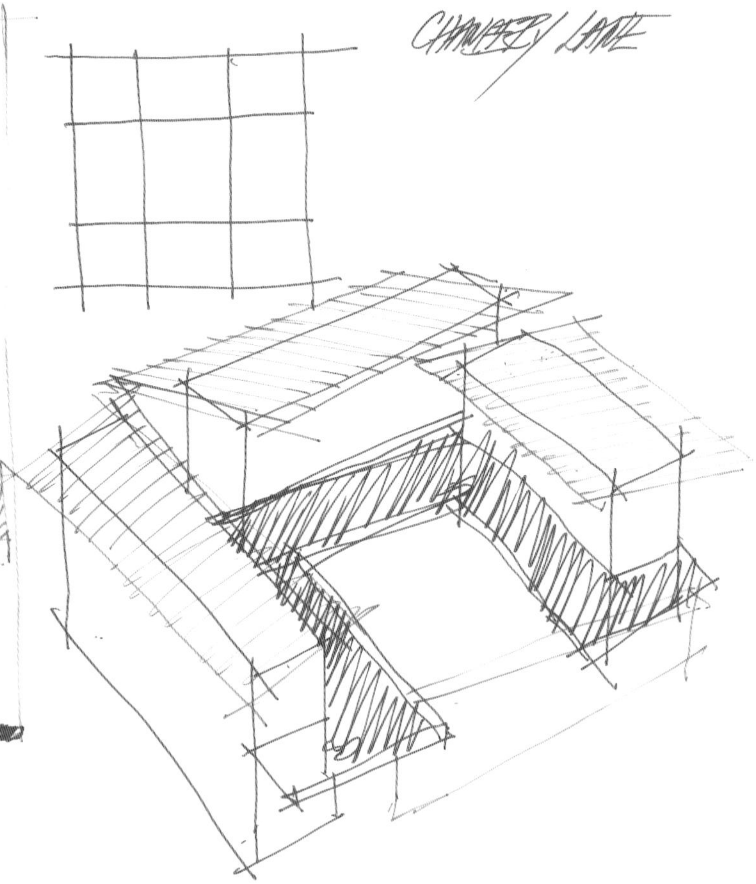

CHAMBERY LANE

022 | DESIGN / SKETCHES

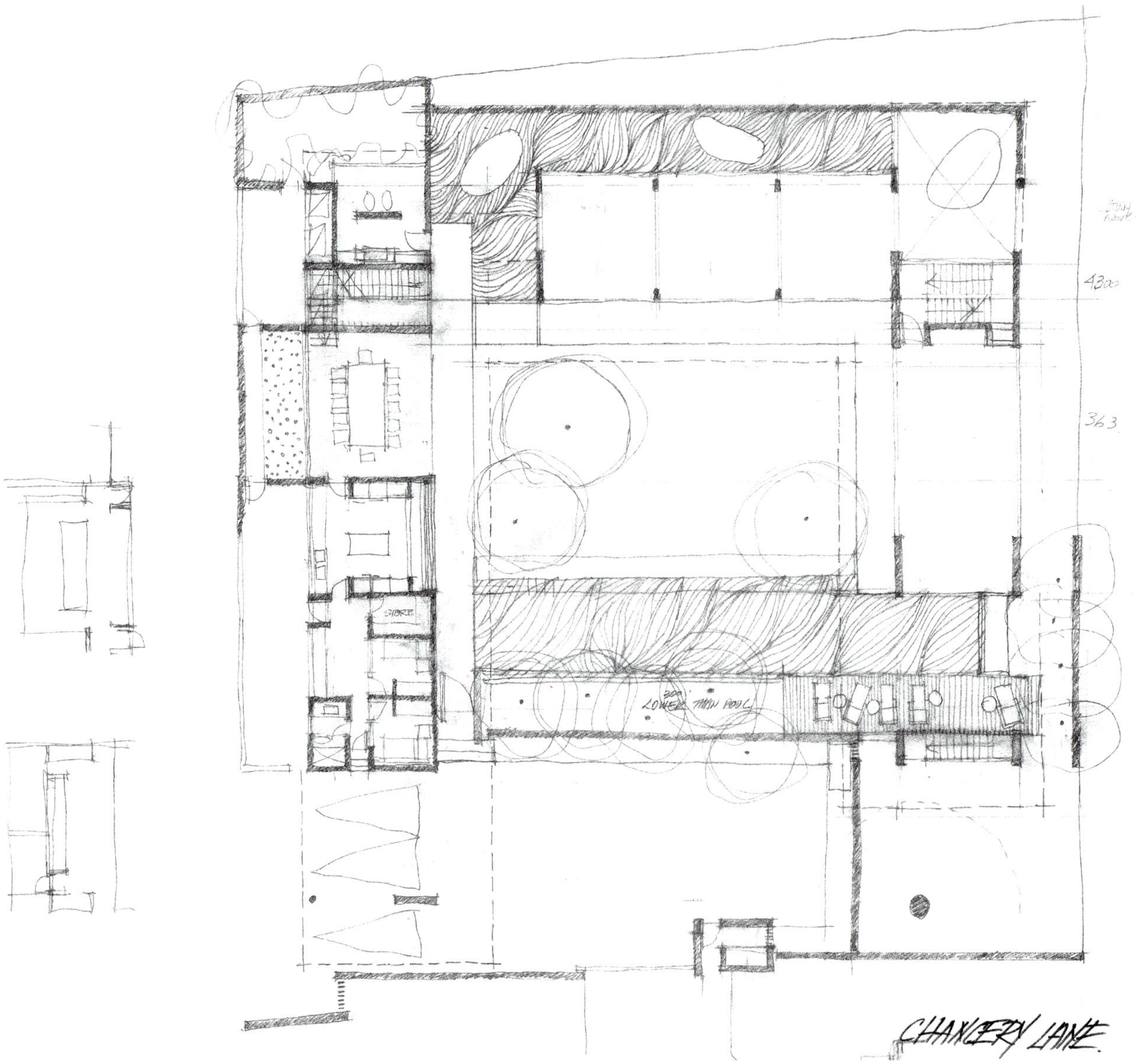

CHANCERY LANE.

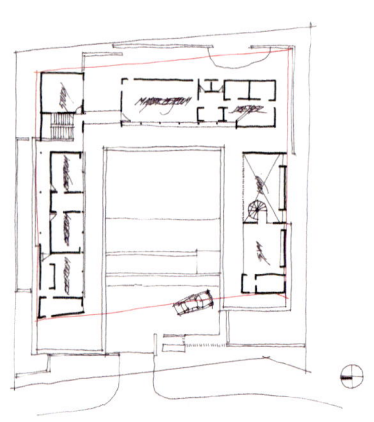 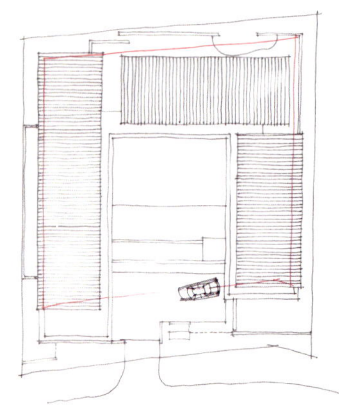 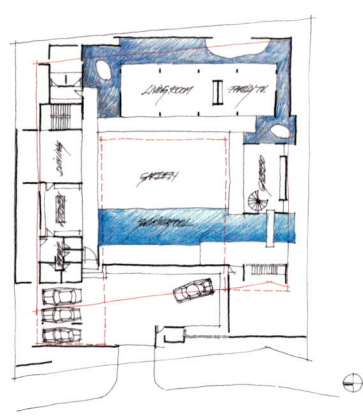

024 | DESIGN / SKETCHES

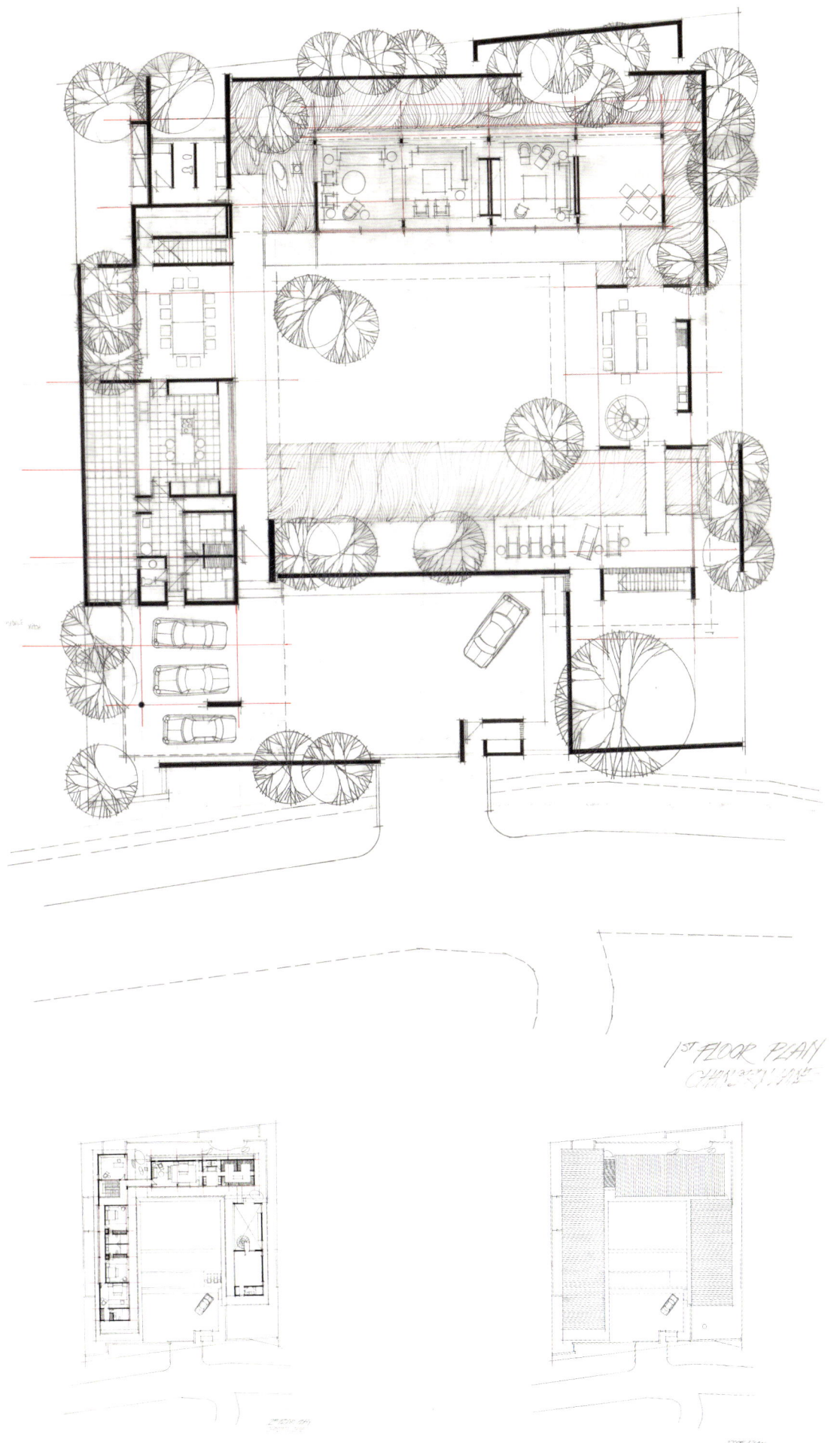

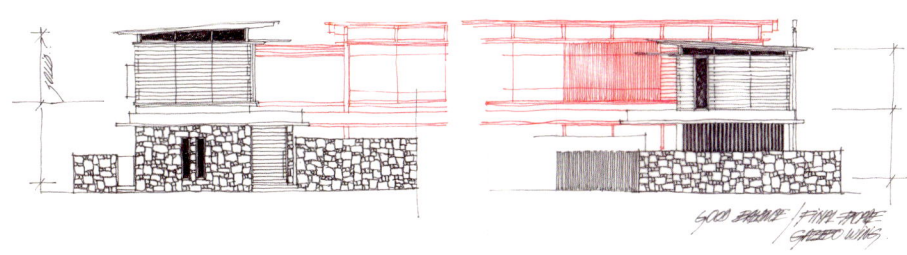

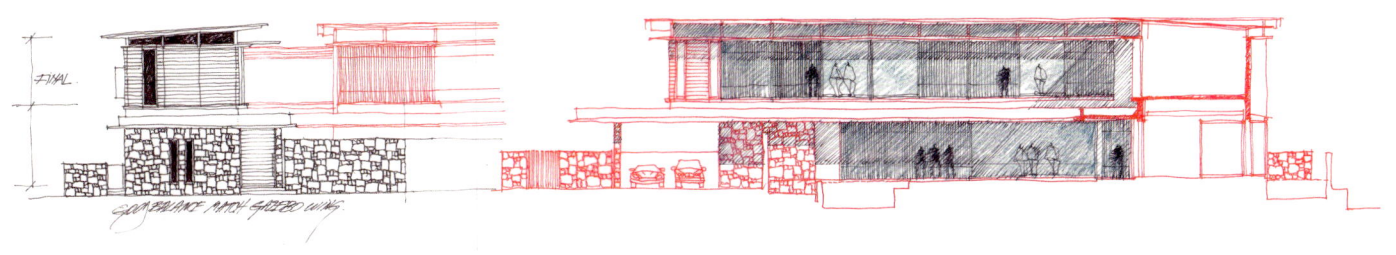

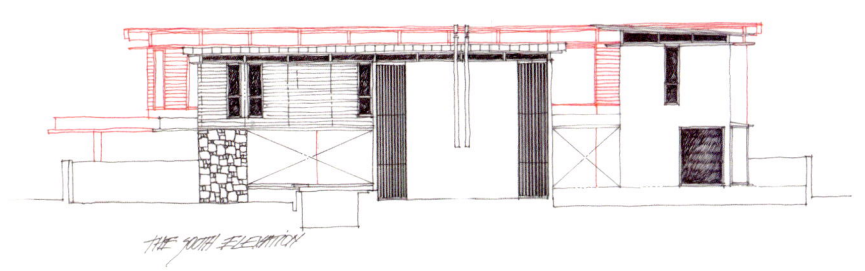

PRESENTATION DRAWINGS

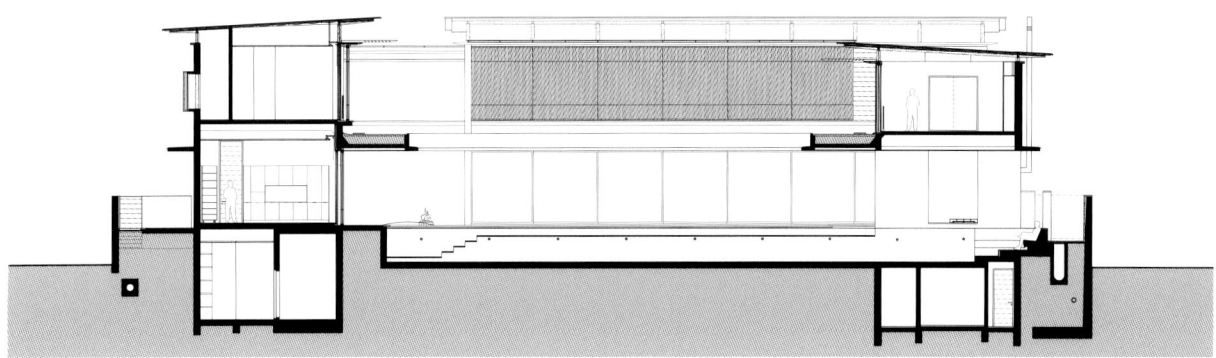

Section A-A

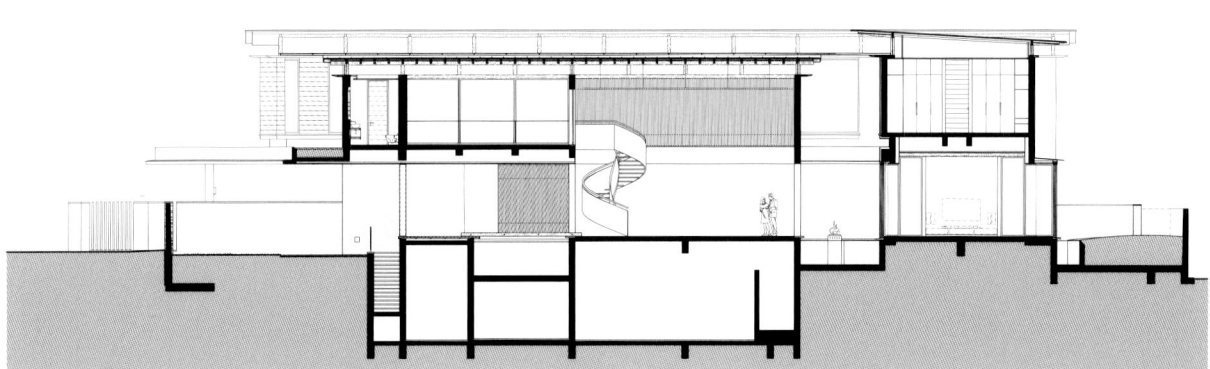

Section B-B

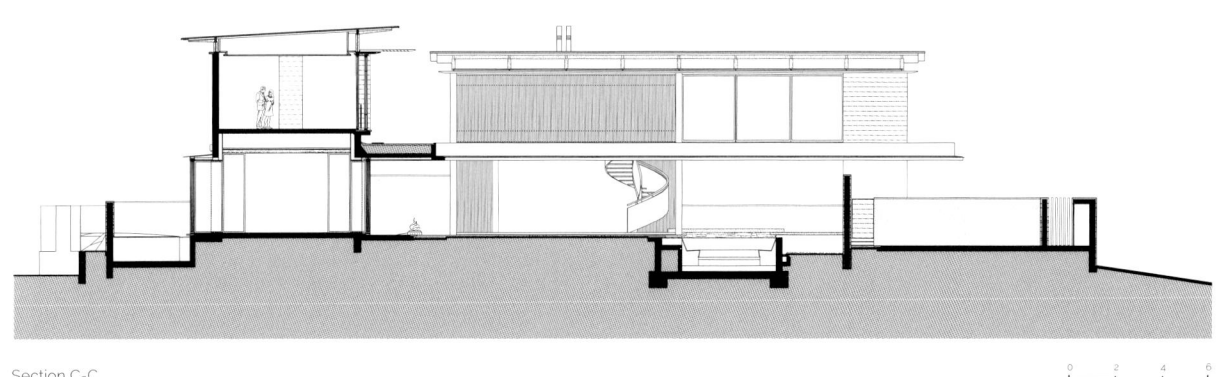

Section C-C

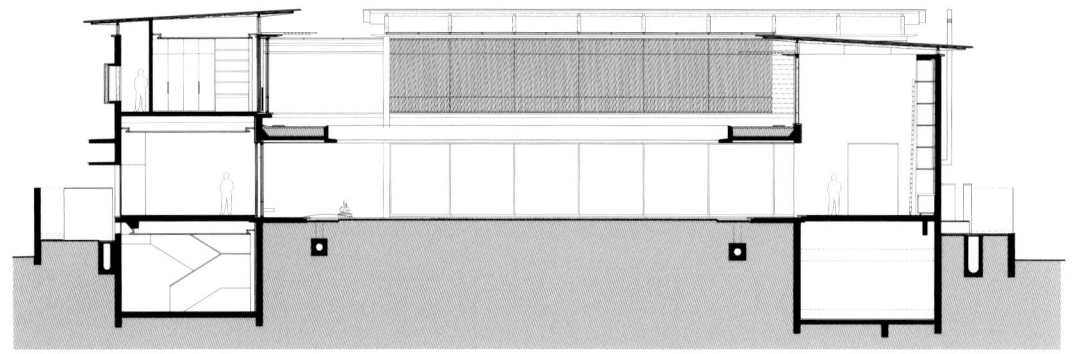

Section D-D

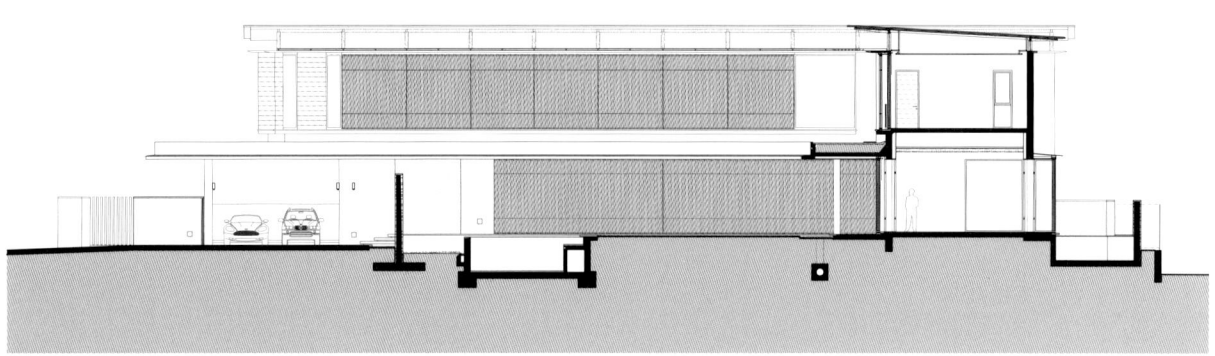

Section E-E

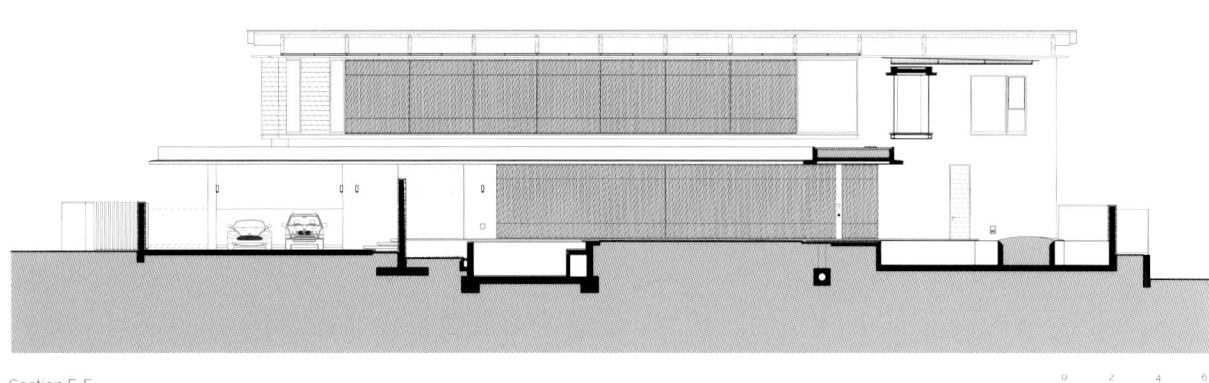

Section F-F

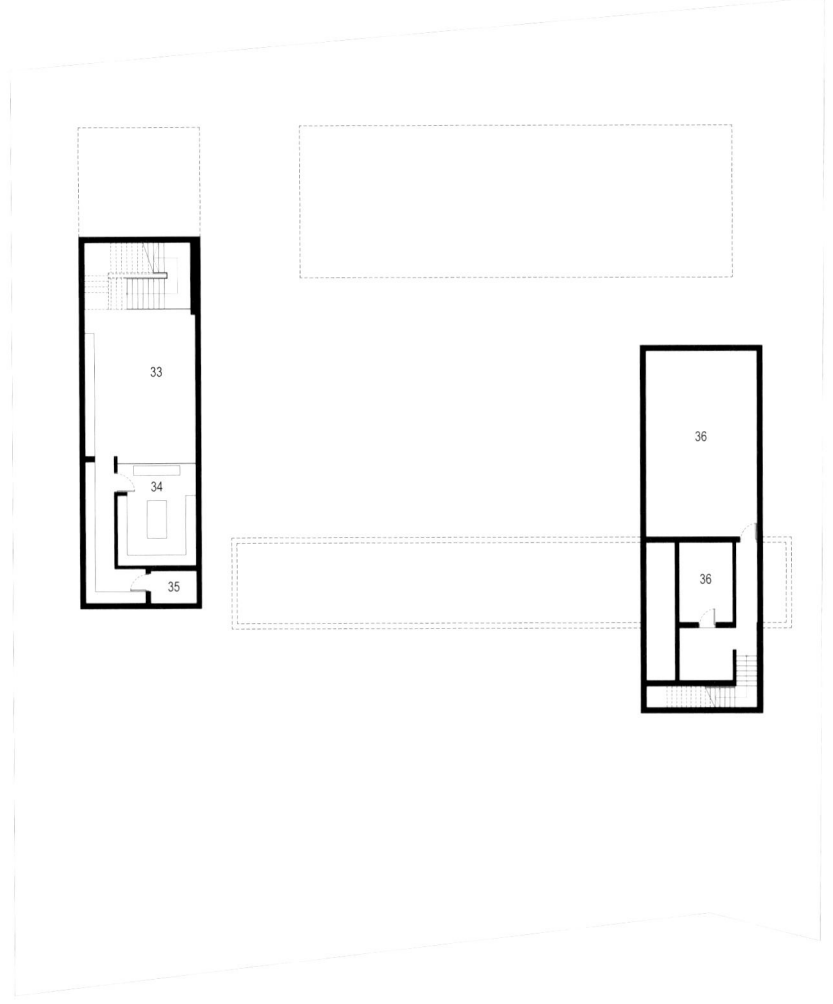

Basement floor plan

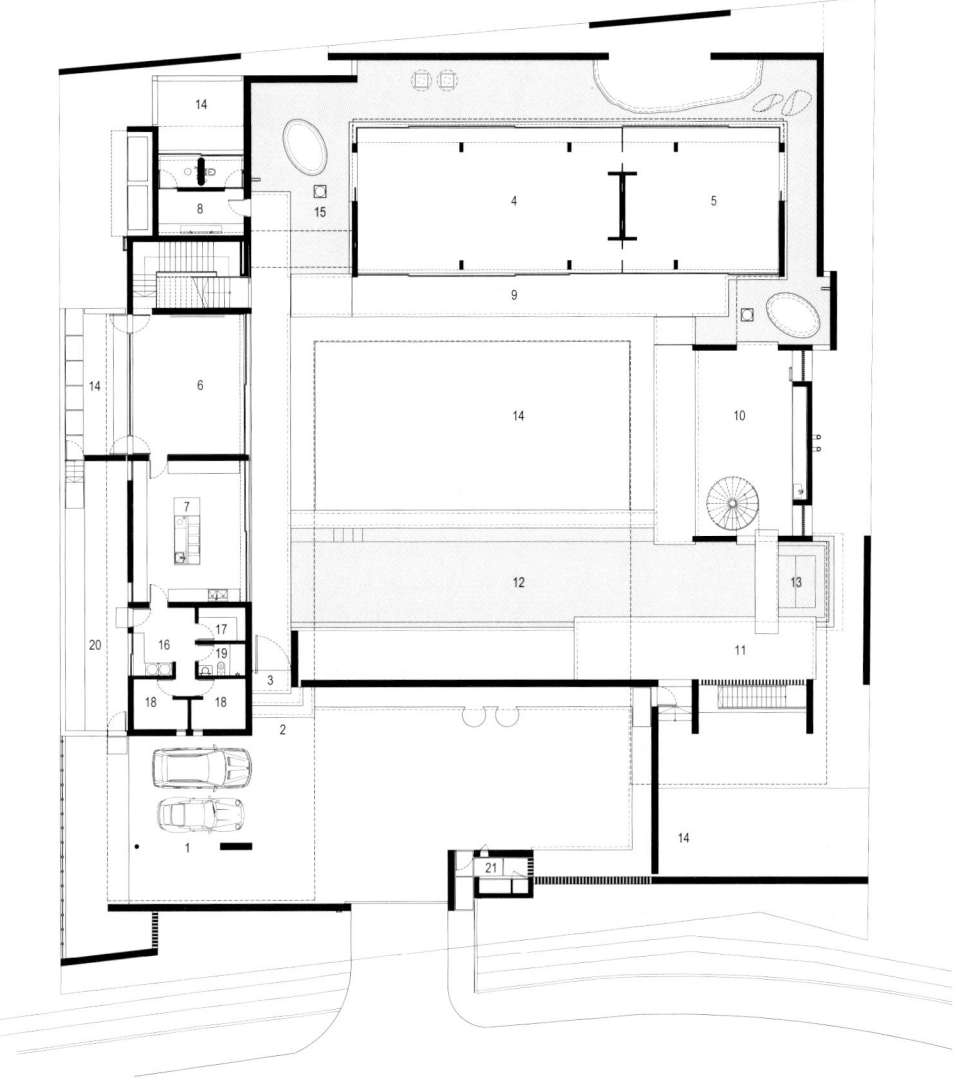

First floor plan

1 Car Porch
2 Entry Drop-Off
3 Entry
4 Living Room
5 Family Room
6 Dining Room
7 Kitchen
8 Powder Room
9 Walkway
10 Outdoor Living / BBQ
11 Pool Deck
12 Swimming Pool
13 Jacuzzi
14 Garden
15 Pond
16 Laundry Room
17 Store Room
18 Maid's Room
19 Maid's Bathroom
20 Service Yard
21 Meter Compartment
33 Games Room
34 Wine Cellar
35 Household Shelter
36 Pool Motor Room

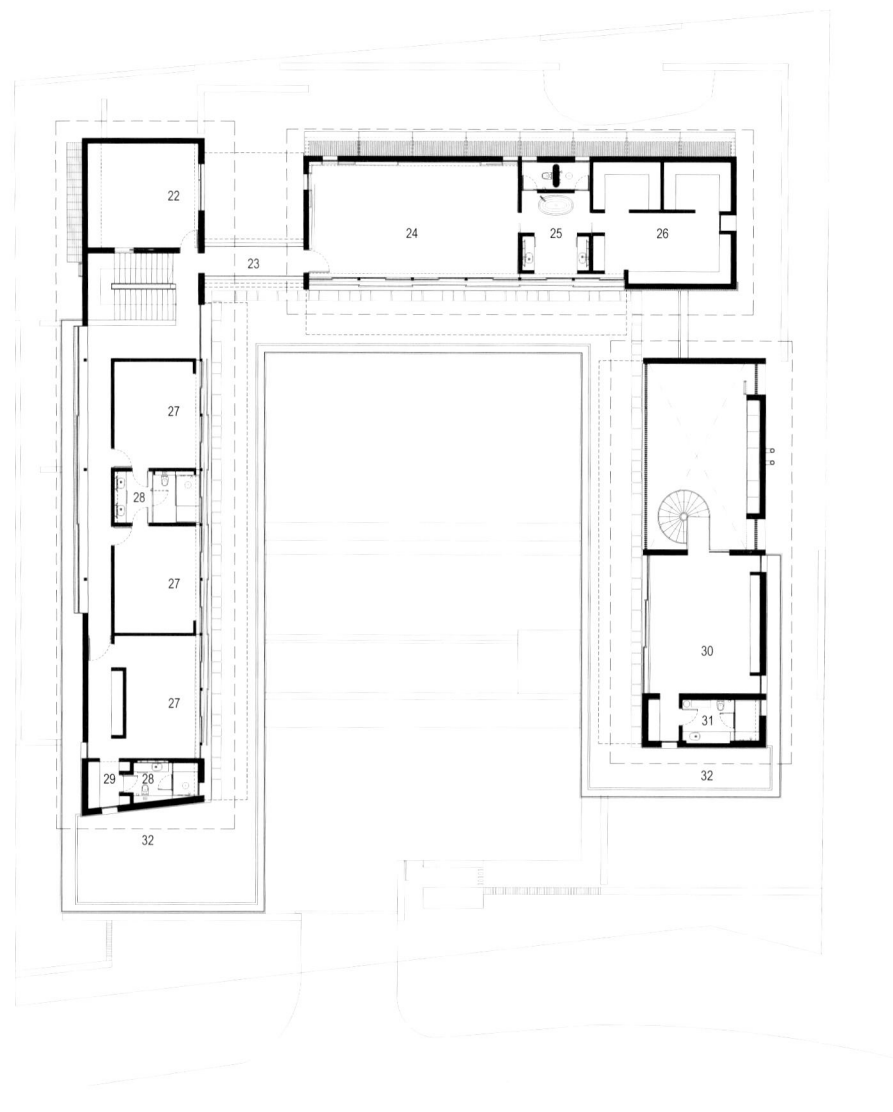

Second floor plan

22 Library
23 Bridge
24 Master Bedroom
25 Master Bathroom
26 Master Dresser
27 Bedroom
28 Bathroom
29 Dresser
30 Gym
31 Gym Bathroom
32 Planter

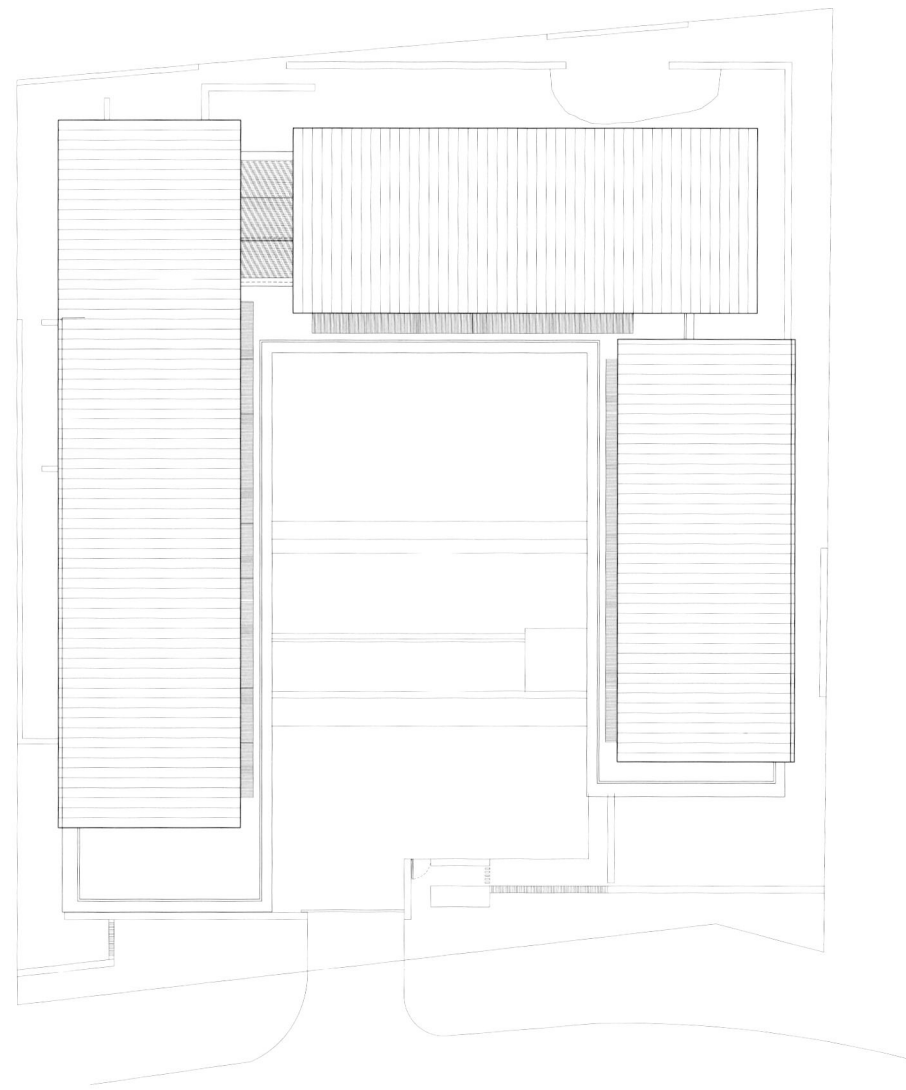

Roof plan

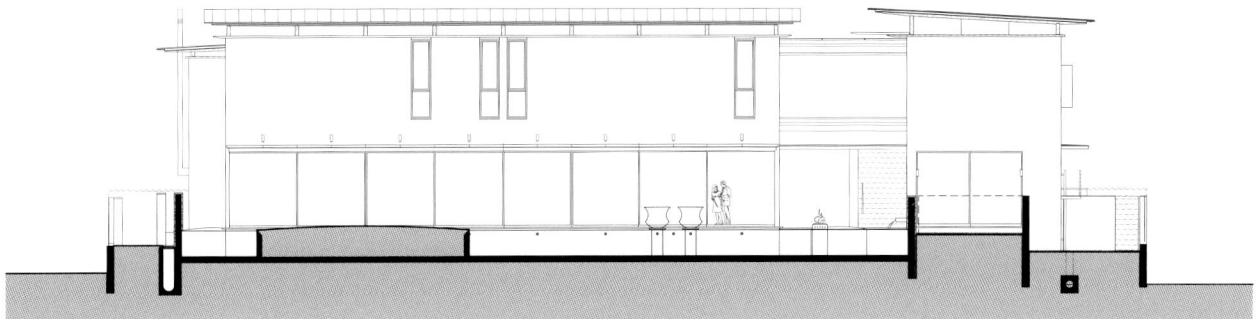
Elevation 1

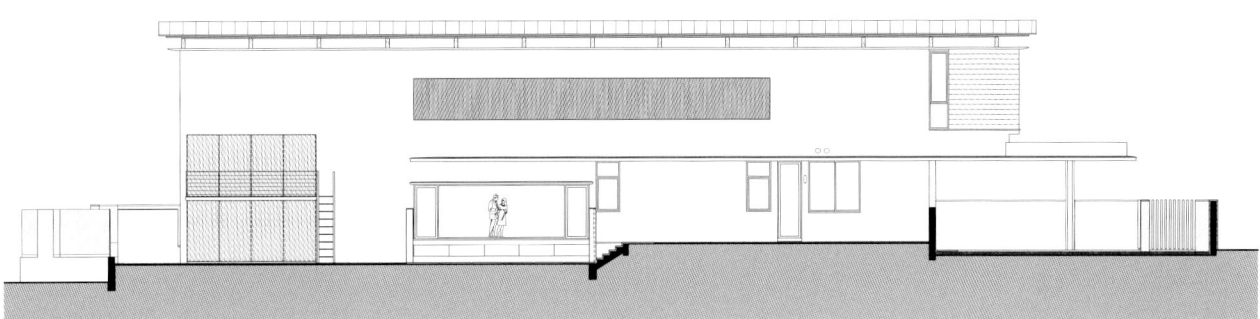
Elevation 2

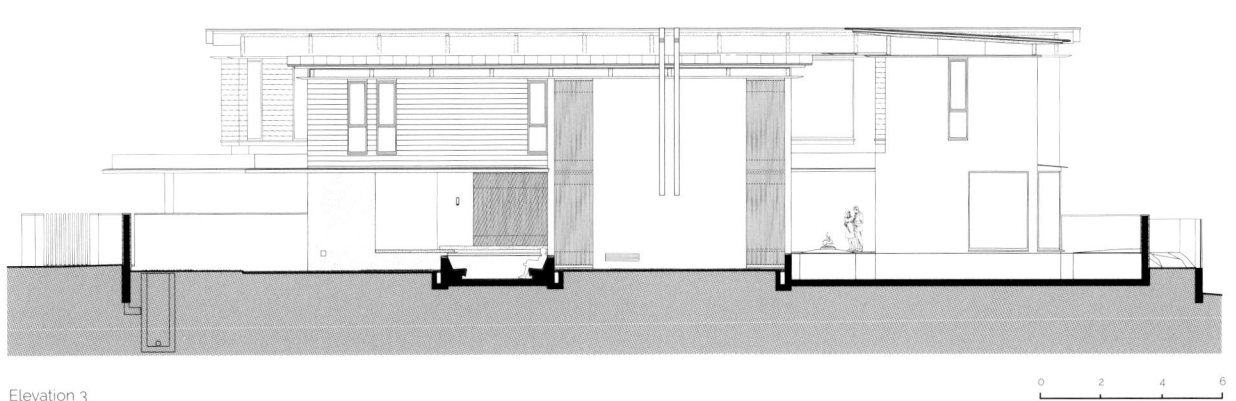
Elevation 3

Elevation 4

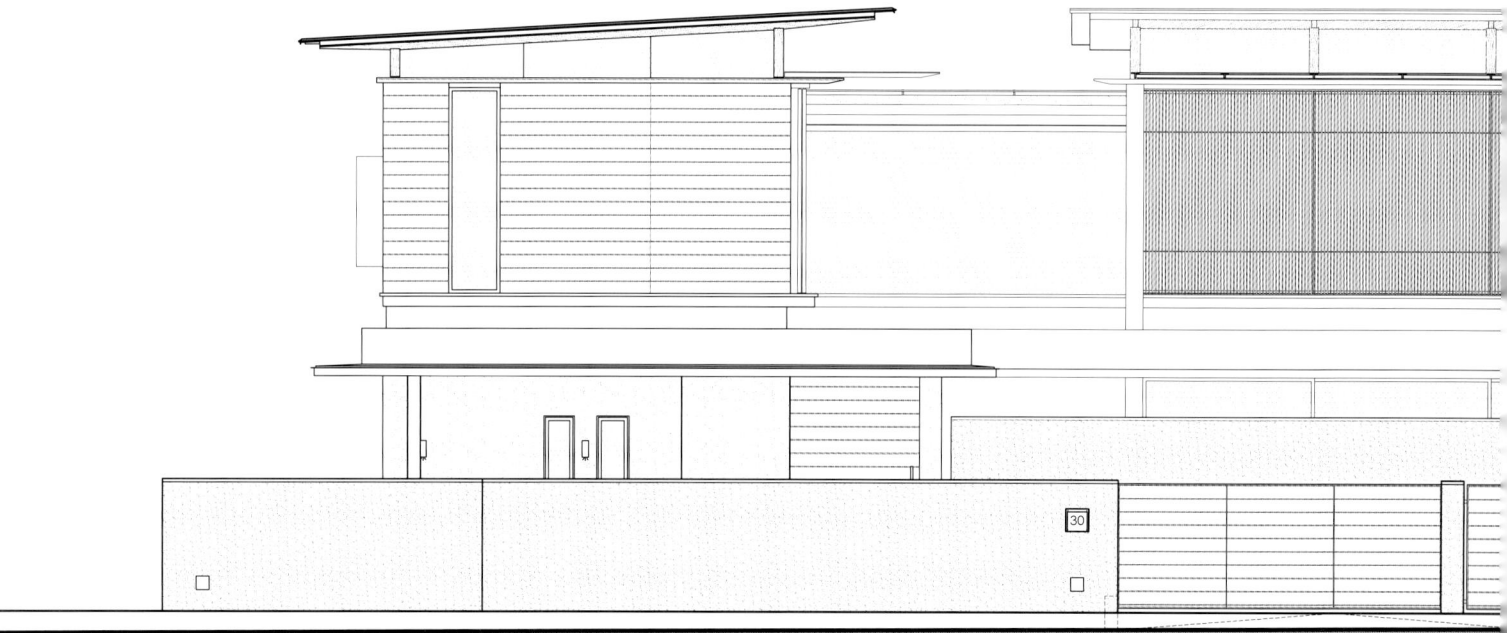

CONSTRUCTION

WORKING DRAWINGS

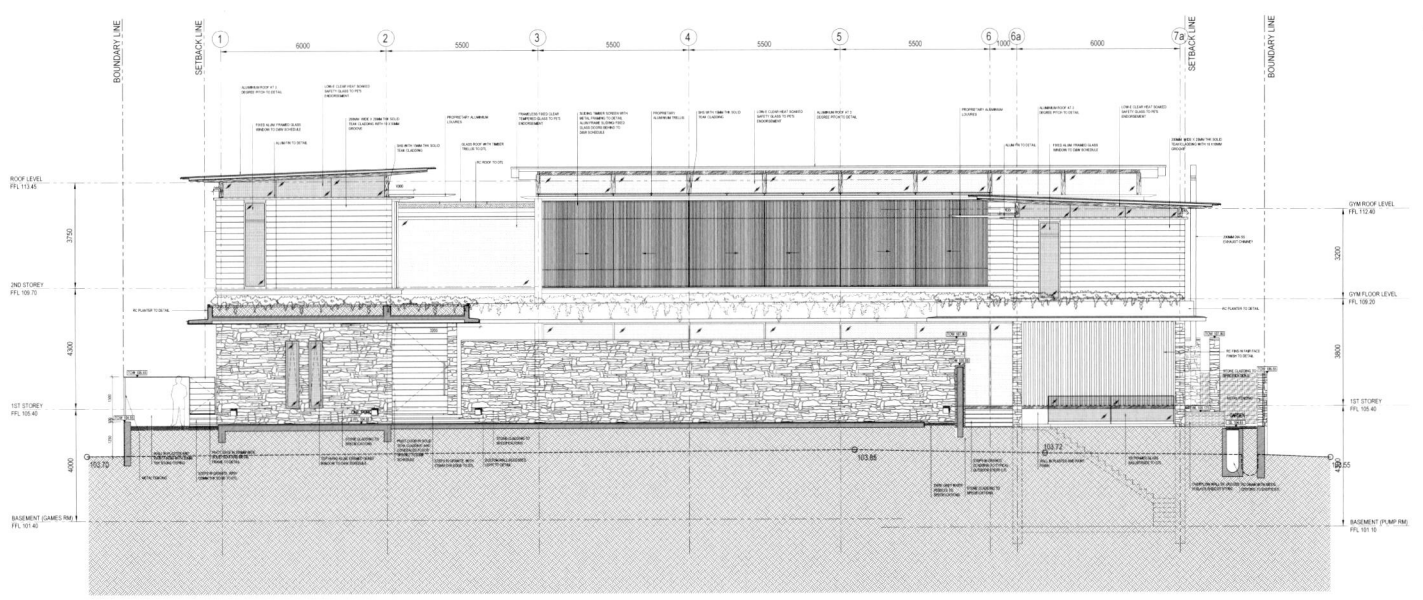

Section A-A

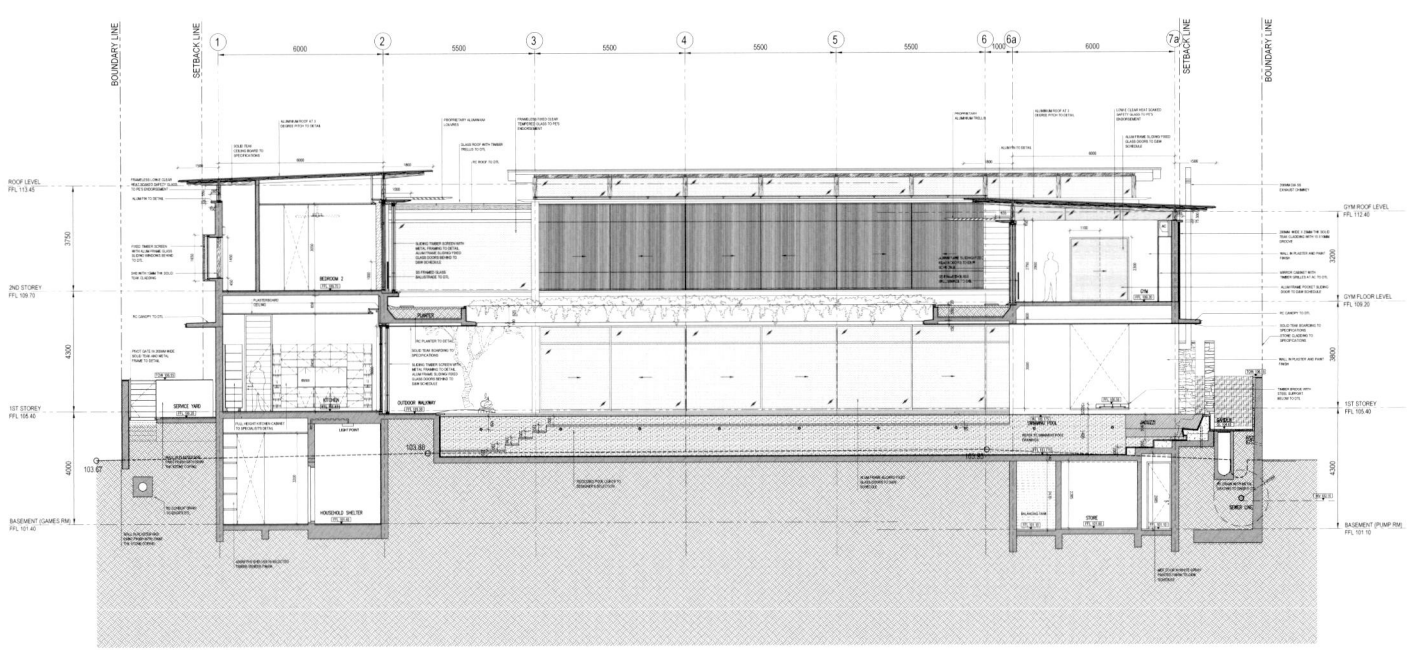

Section B-B

Section G-G

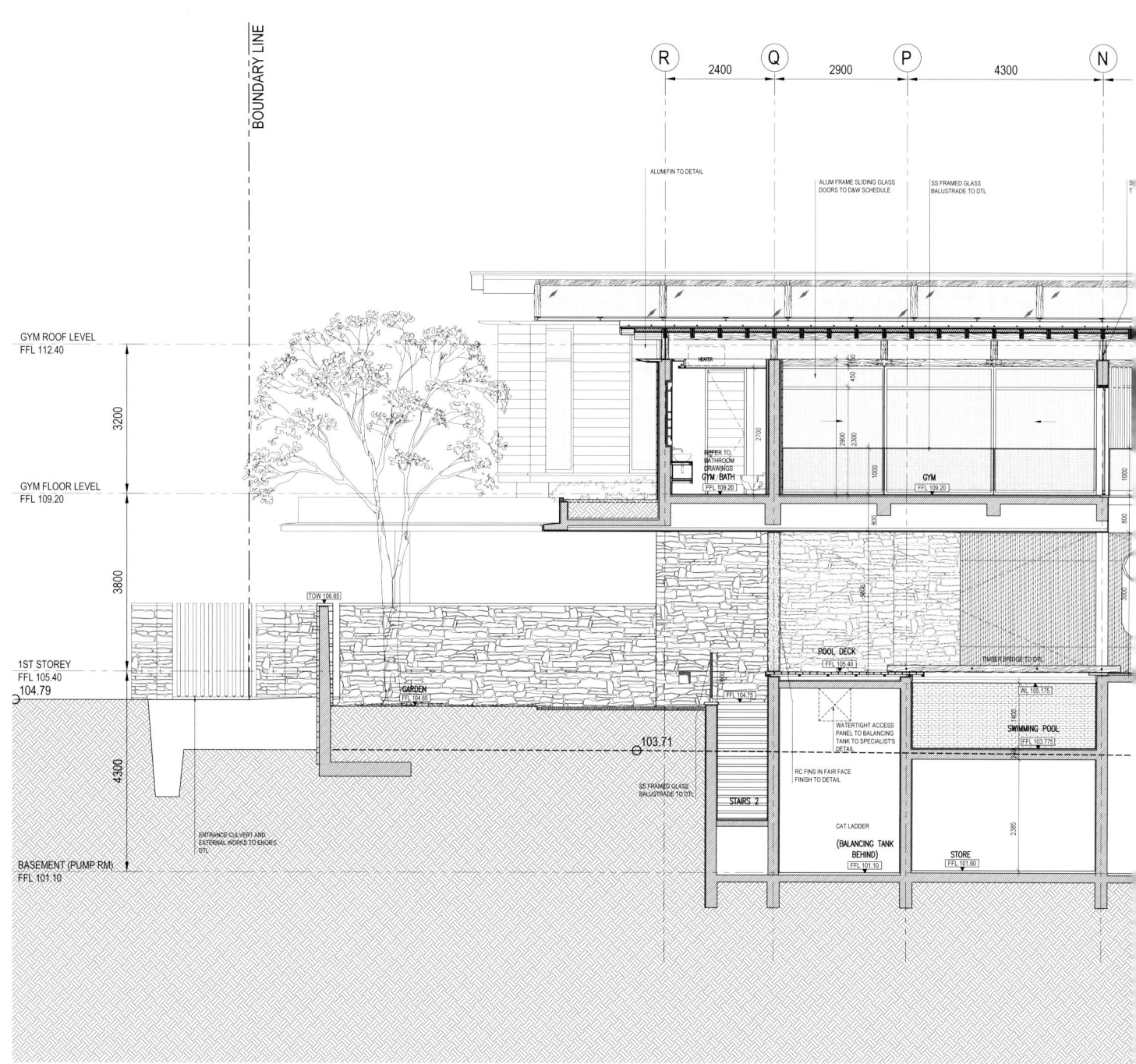

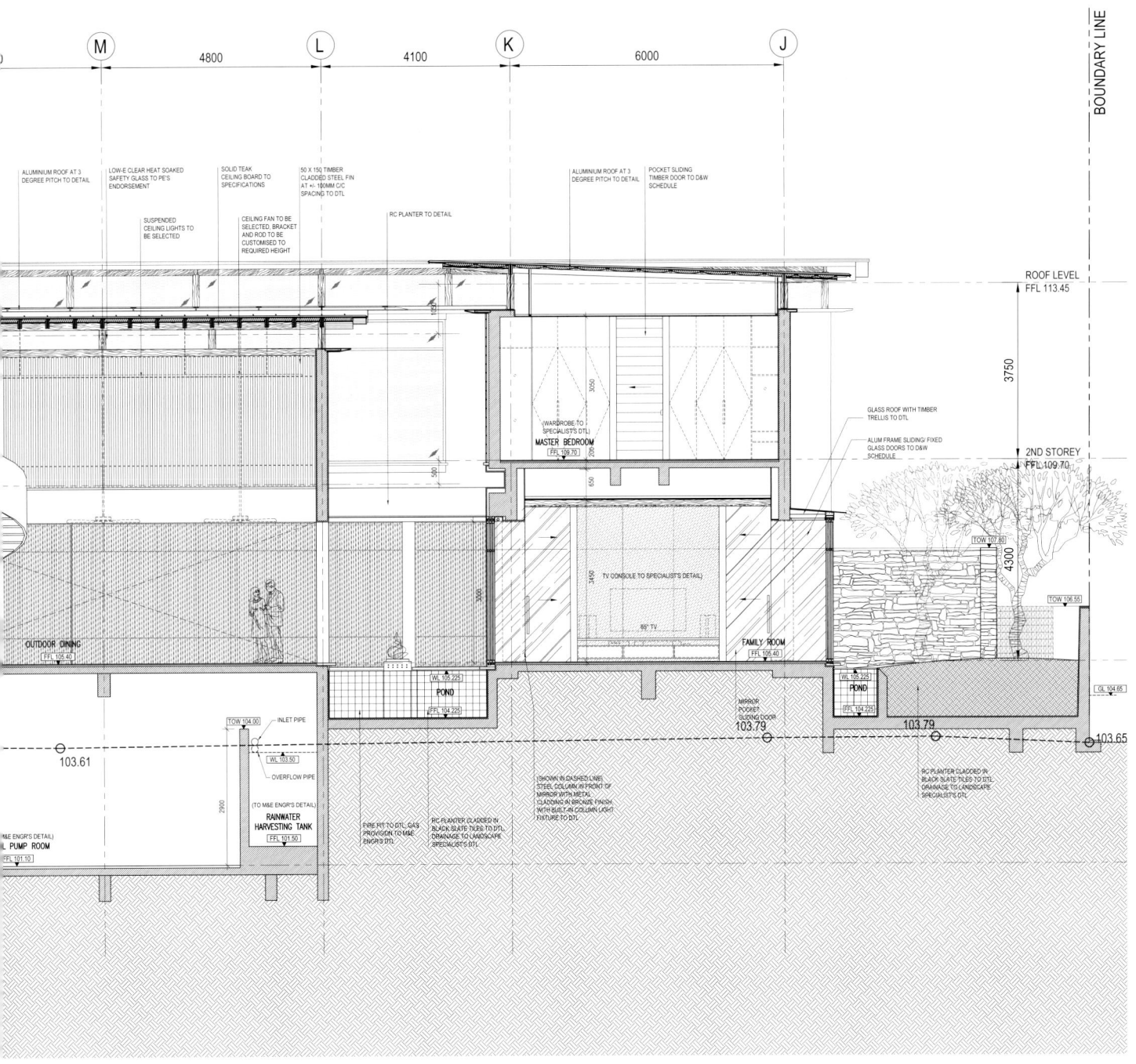

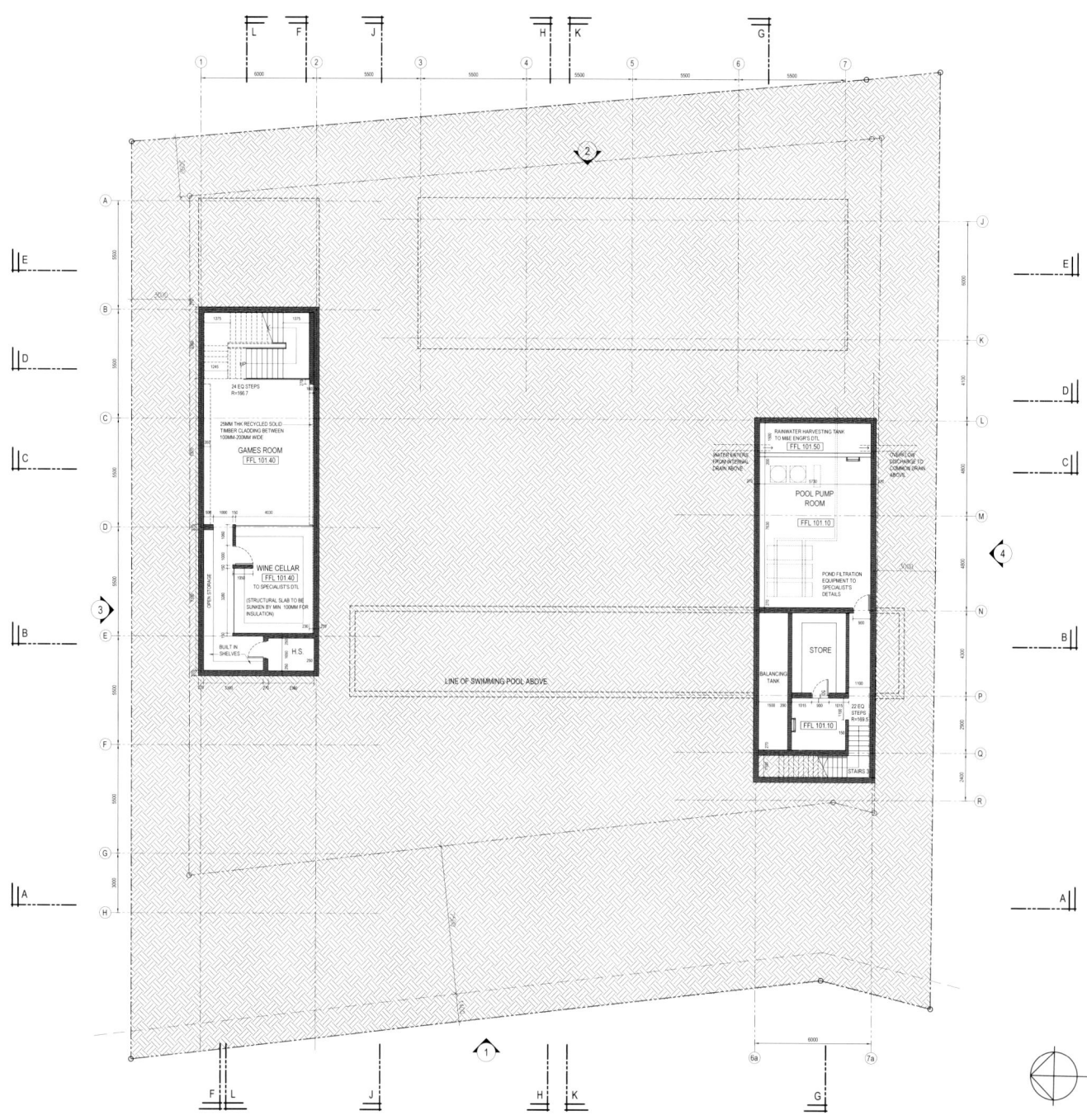

Setting Out Plans - Basement

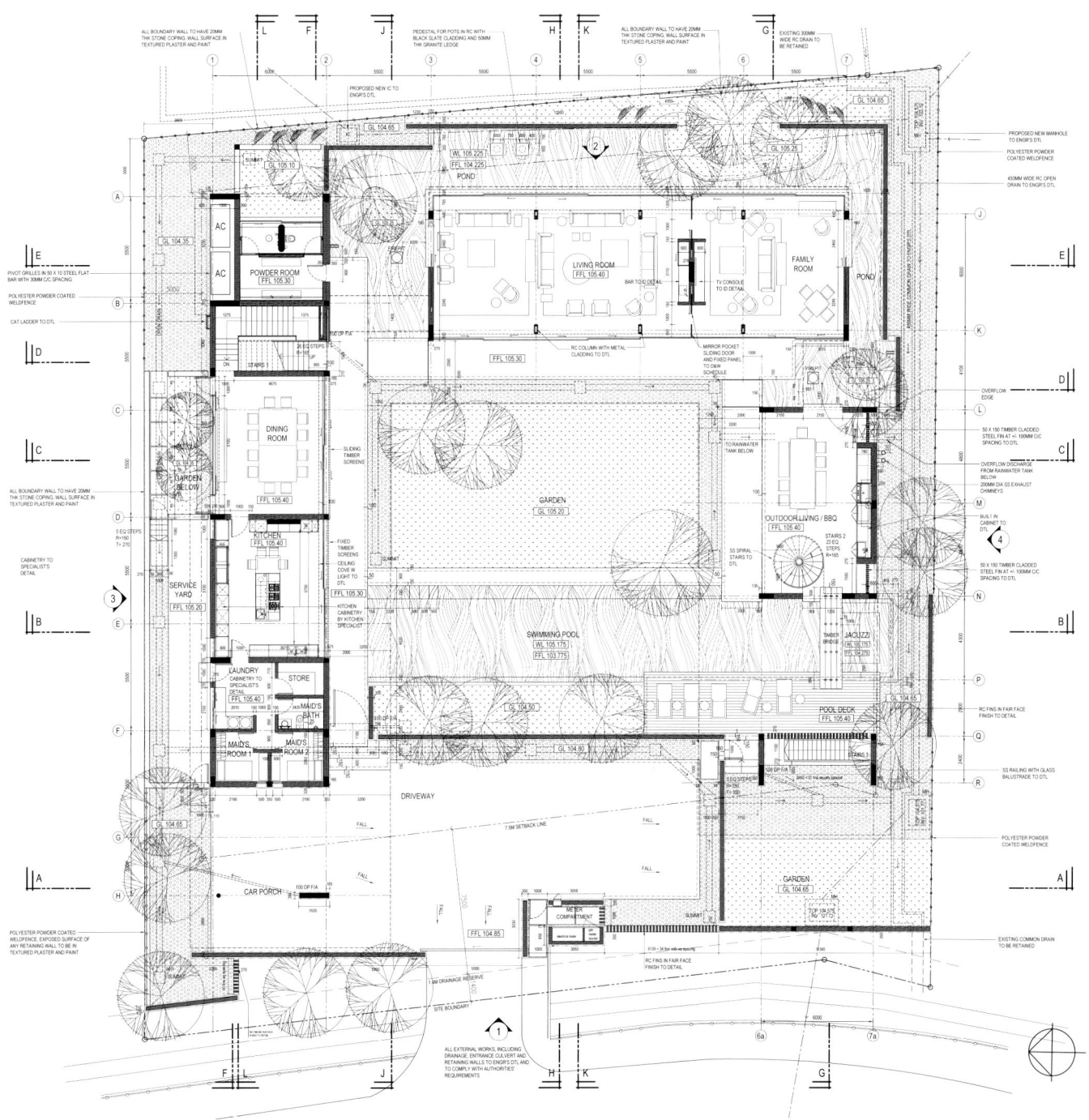

Setting Out Plans - First Storey

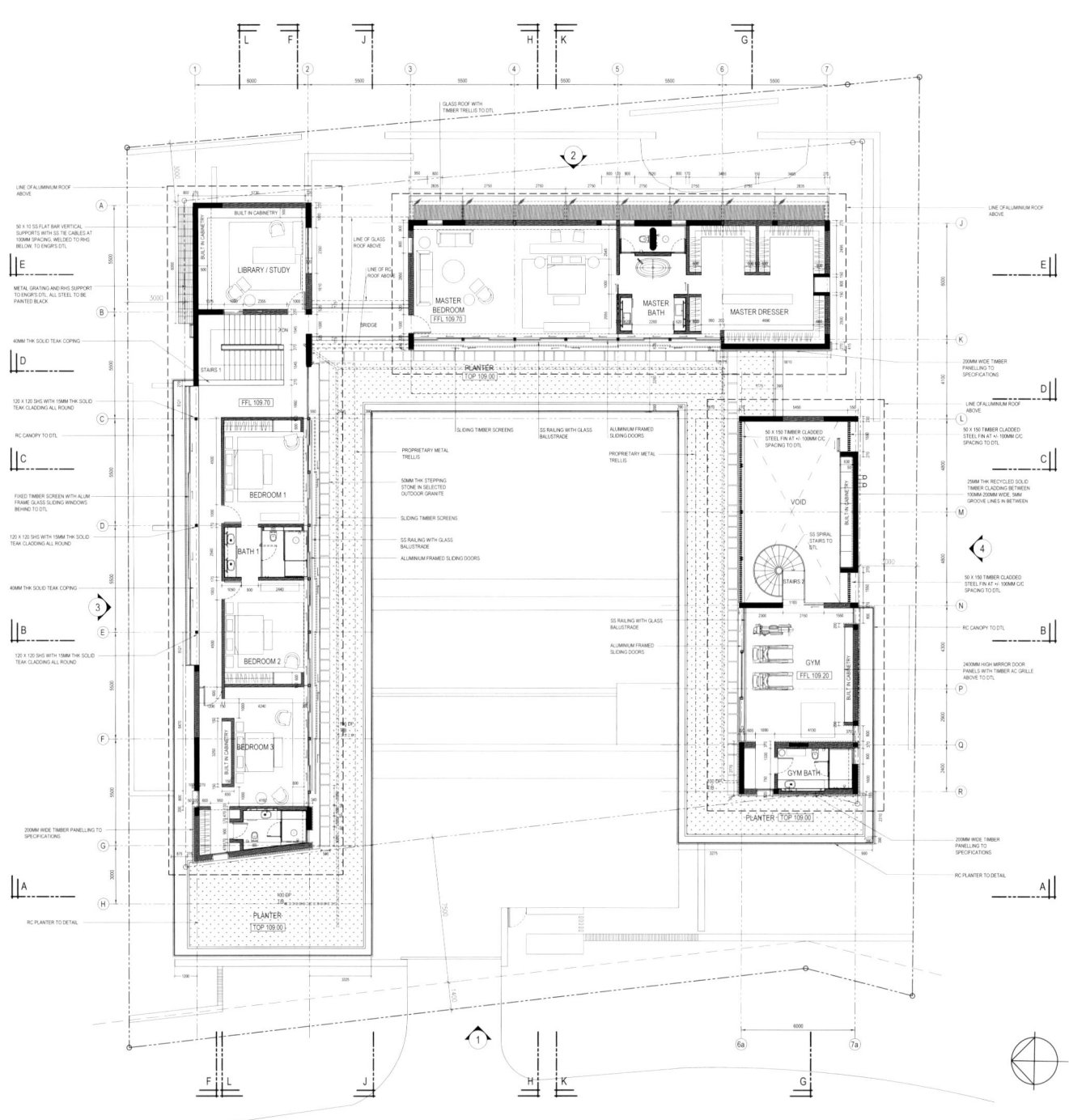

Setting Out Plans - Second Storey

048 | CONSTRUCTION / WORKING DRAWINGS

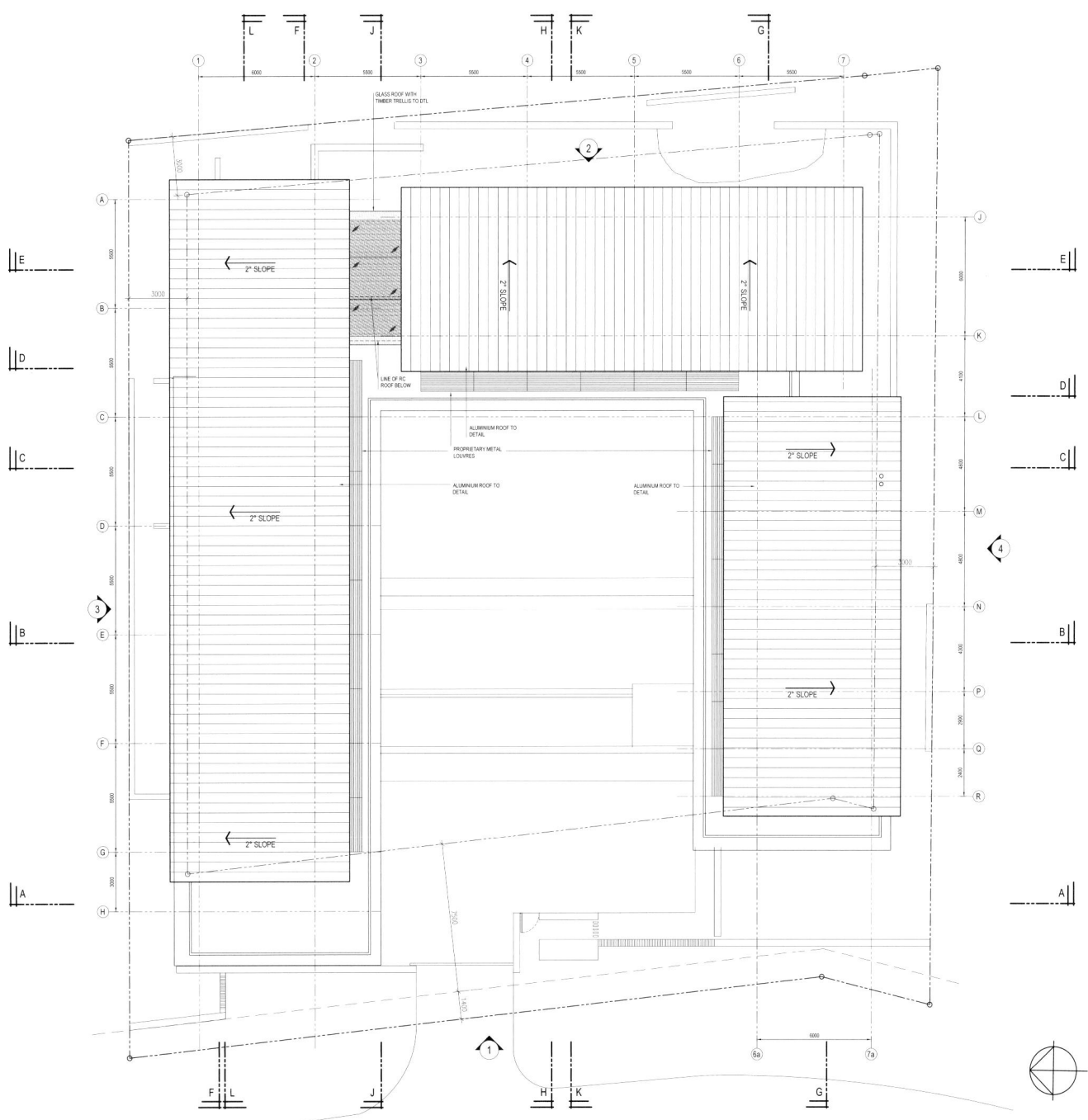

Setting Out Plans - Plan

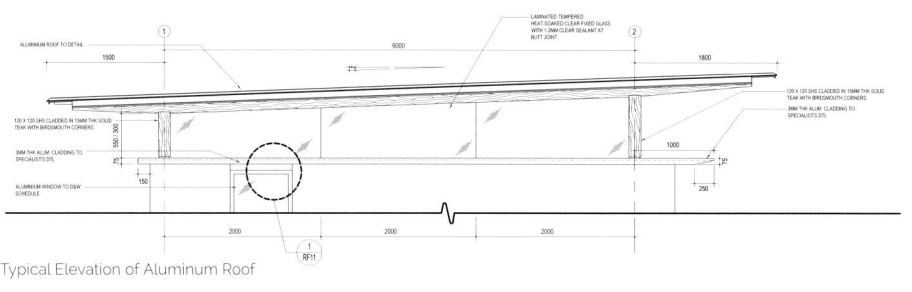

Typical Elevation of Aluminum Roof

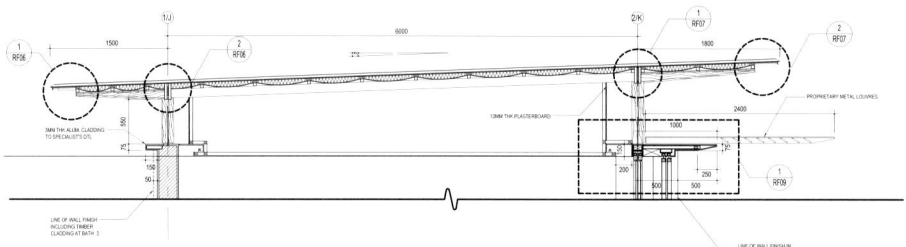

Roof Section at Bedroom 1/2/3 & Master Bedroom

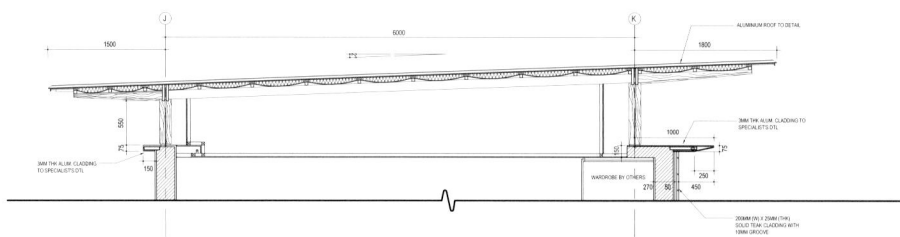

Roof Section at Master Dresser

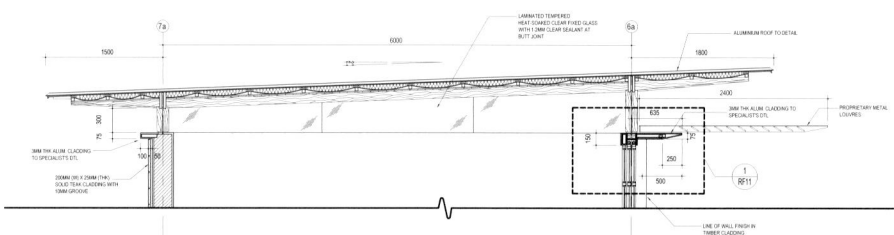

Roof Section at Gym

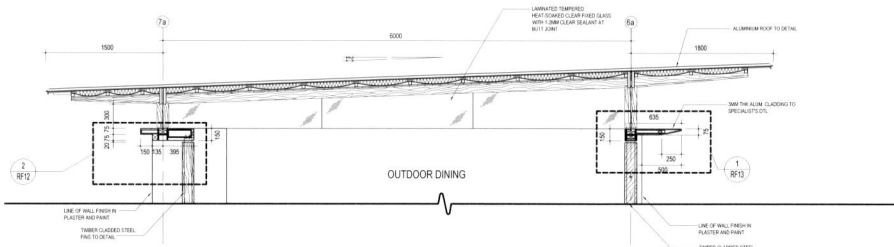

Roof Section at Outdoor Dining (through timber fins)

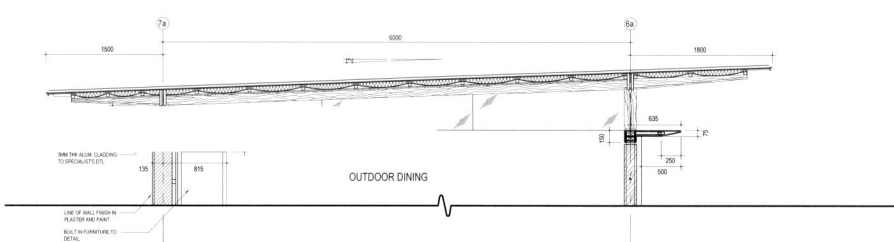

Roof Section at Outdoor Dining (through cabinetry)

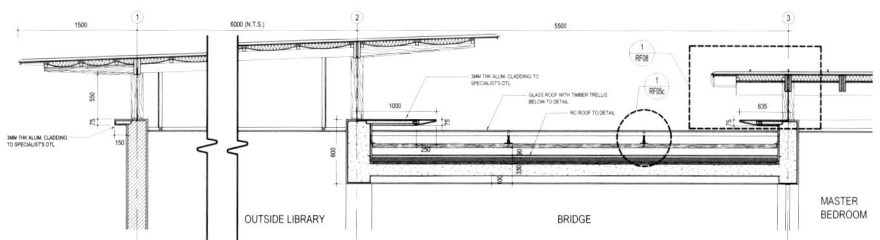

Roof Section at Bridge between Library and Master Bedroom

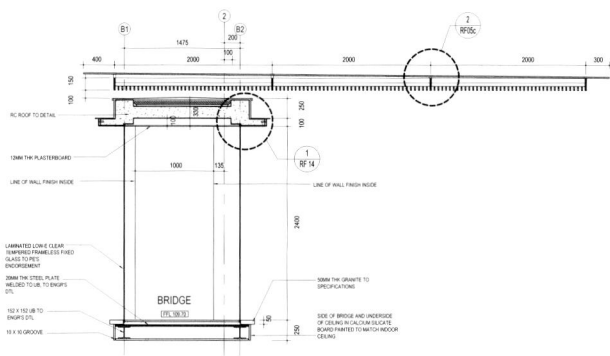

Roof Section at Bridge between Library and Master Bedroom

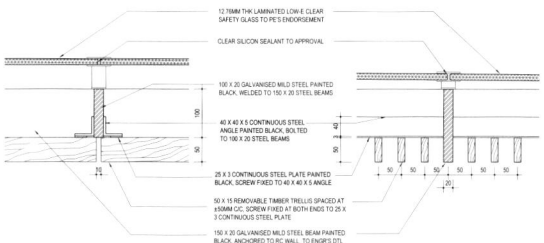

Trail Detail Sections

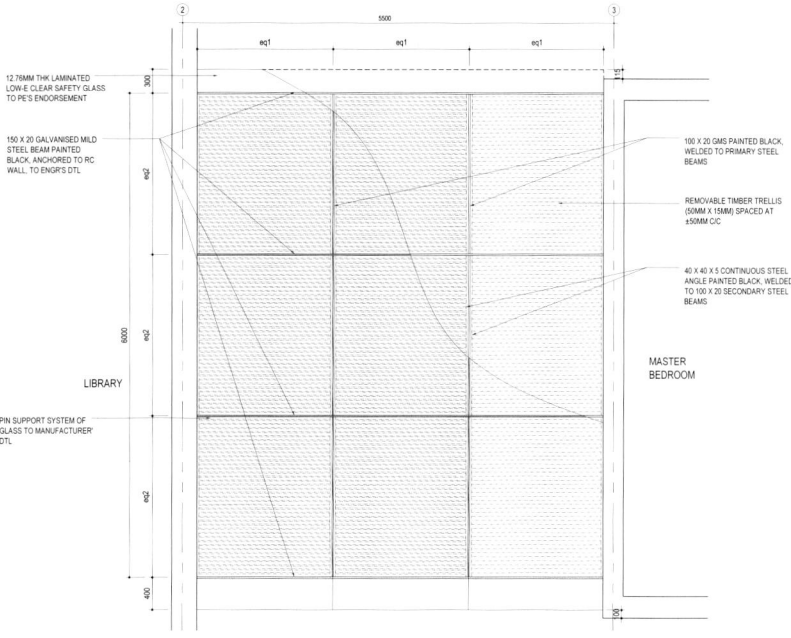

Glass Roof and Timber Trellis Plan

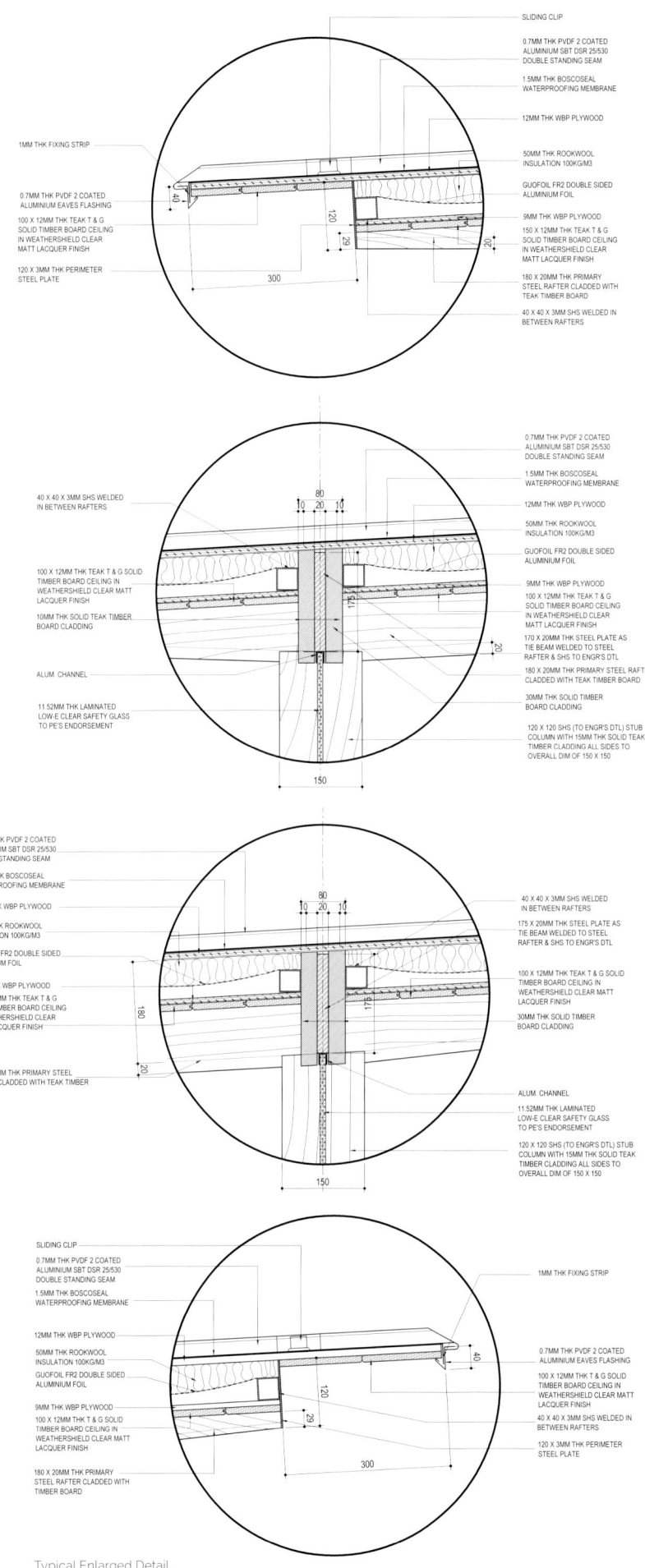

Typical Enlarged Detail

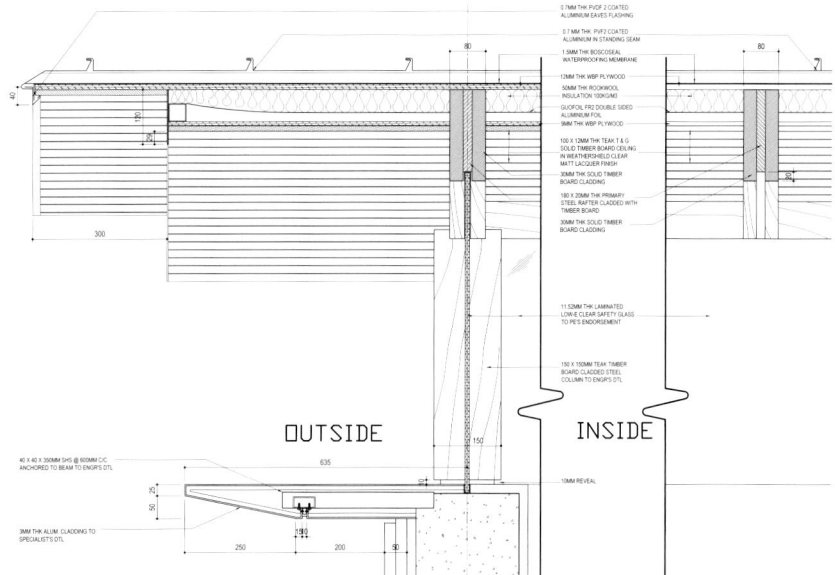

Typical Enlarged Detail

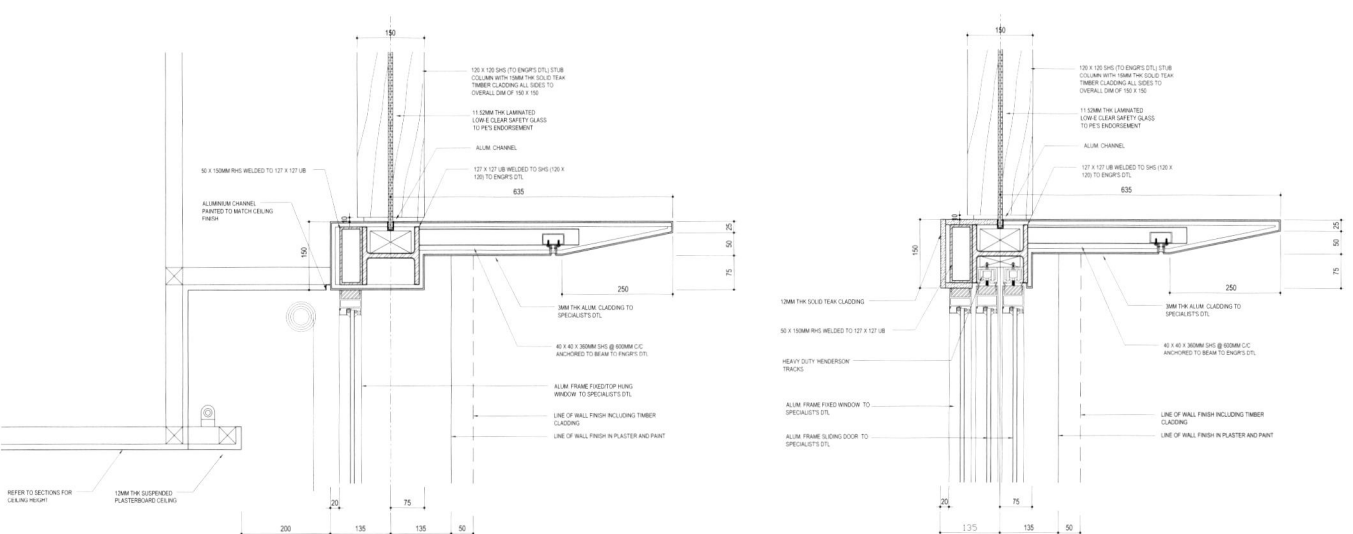

Typical Fixed/Top Hung Window Head Detail

Gym Sliding Door - Doors Head Detail

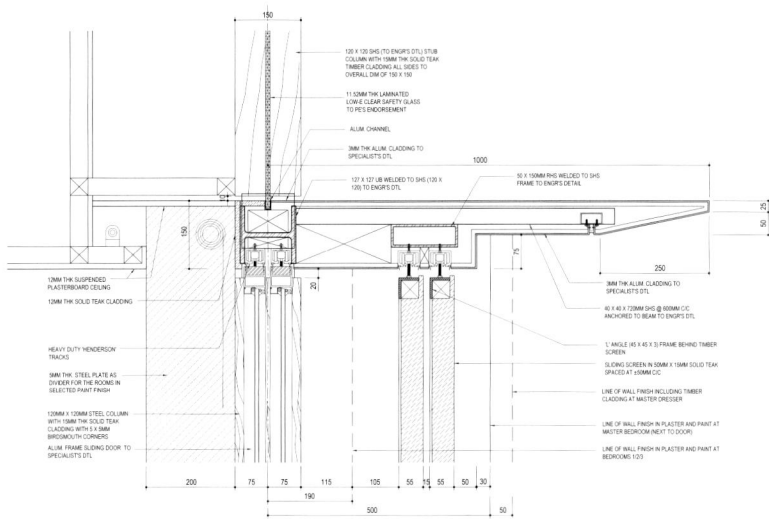

Typical Sliding Doors with Timber Screen Detail - Bedrooms 1/2/3 /Master

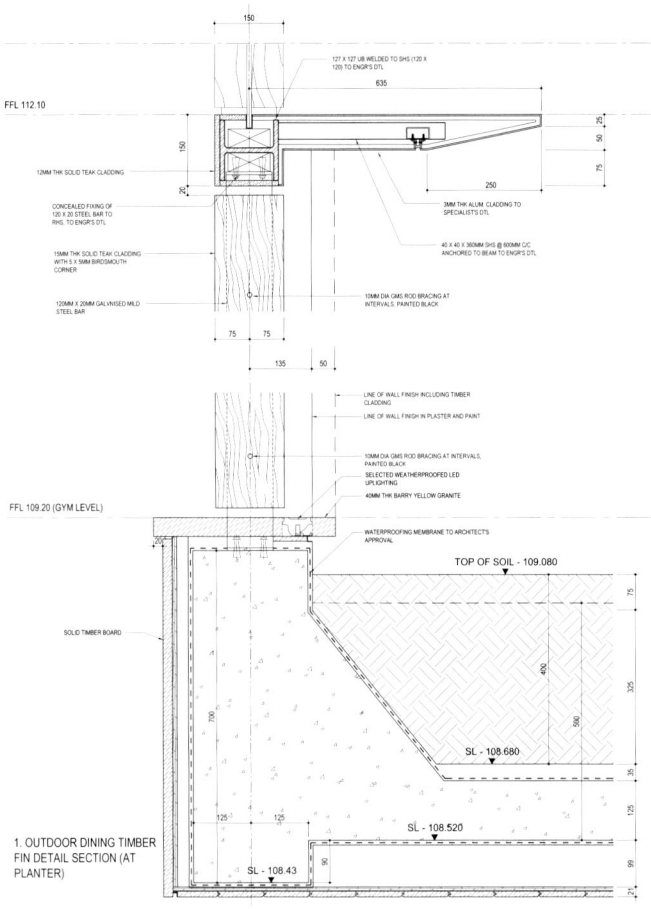

Outdoor Dining Timber Fin Detail Section (at Planter)

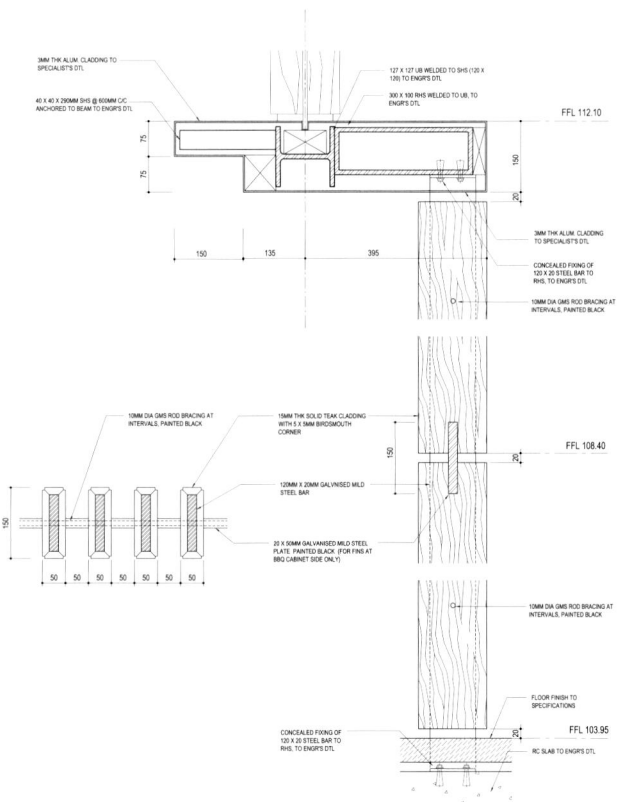

Outdoor Dining Timber Fin - Detail Plan & Detail Section (at BBQ Cabinet)

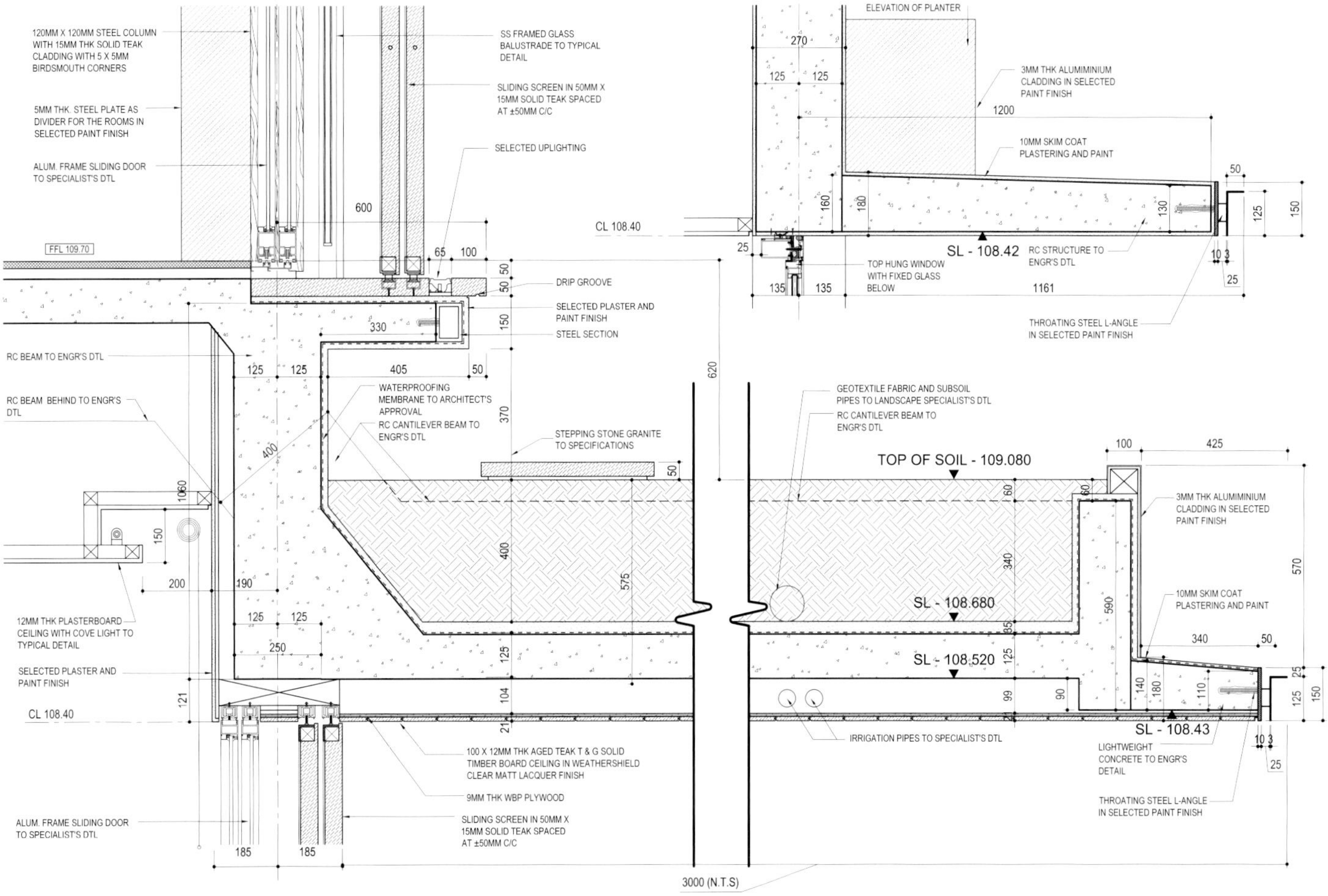

Typical Roof Planter Detail at Dining BLock & RC Canopy Detail at Kitchen

RC Roof at Bridge Detail

Typical Roof Planter Detail at Living Block

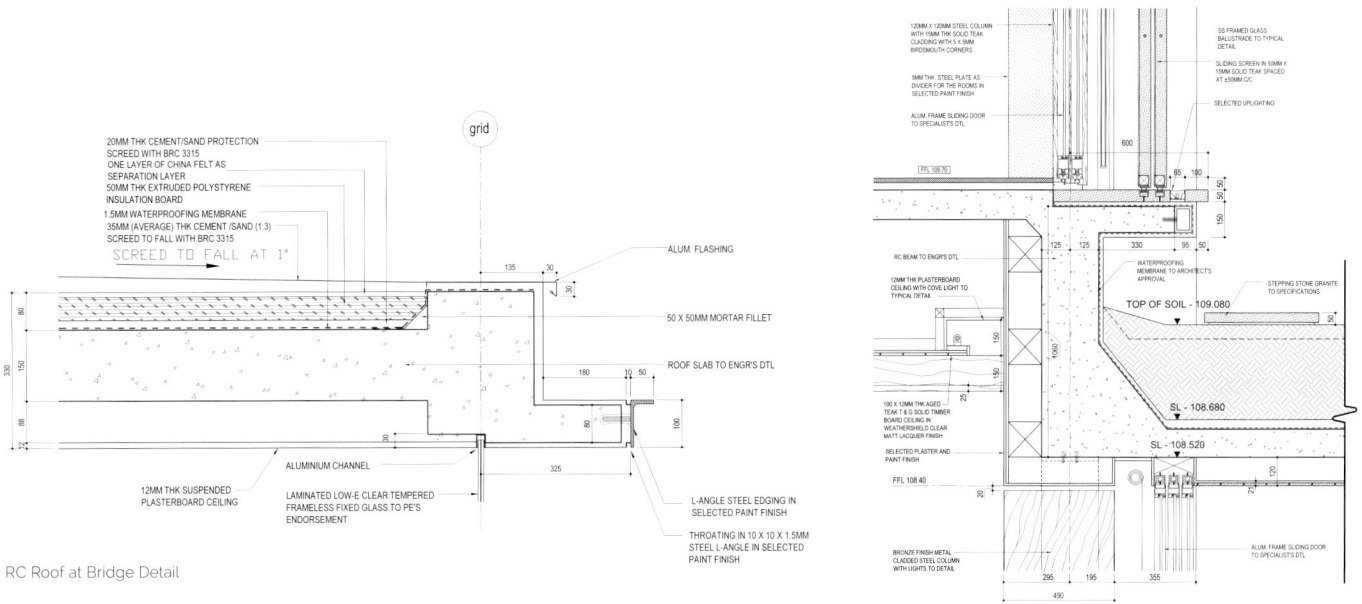

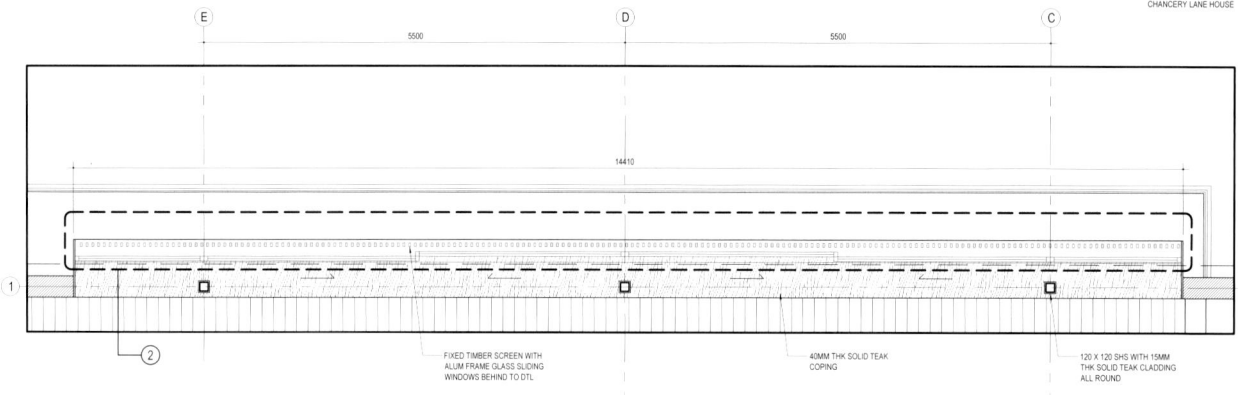

Second Floor Part Plan - Bedroom Corridor

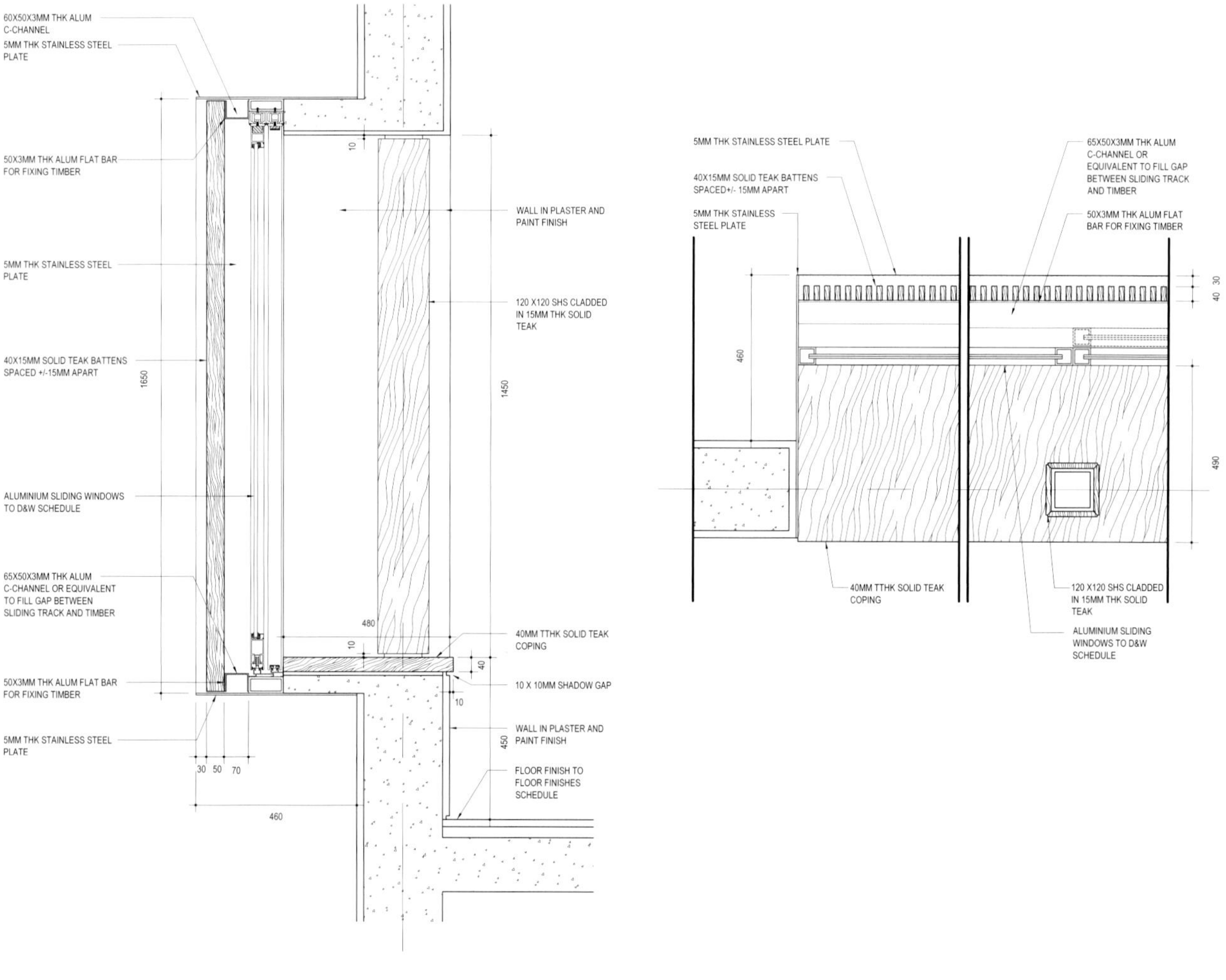

Fixed Timber Screen Detail at Second Floor Bedroom Corridor - Elevation & Plan

Elevation - Fixed Timber Screen Detail at Second Floor Bedroom Corridor

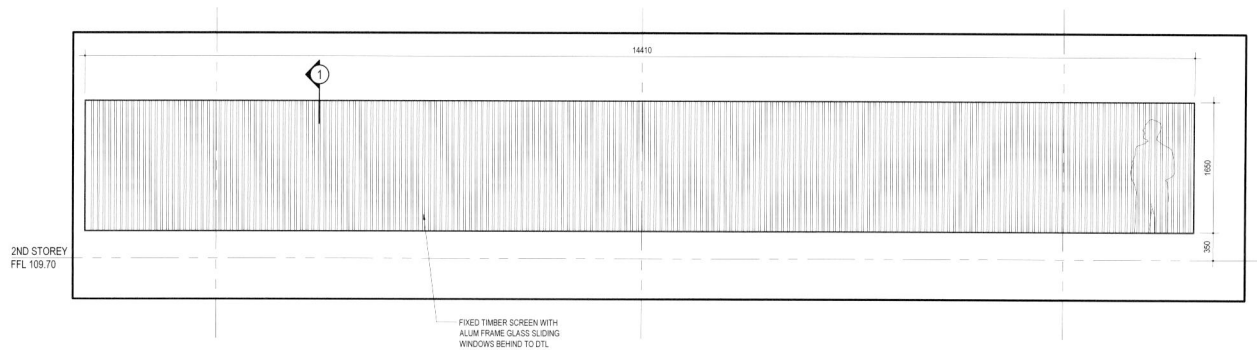

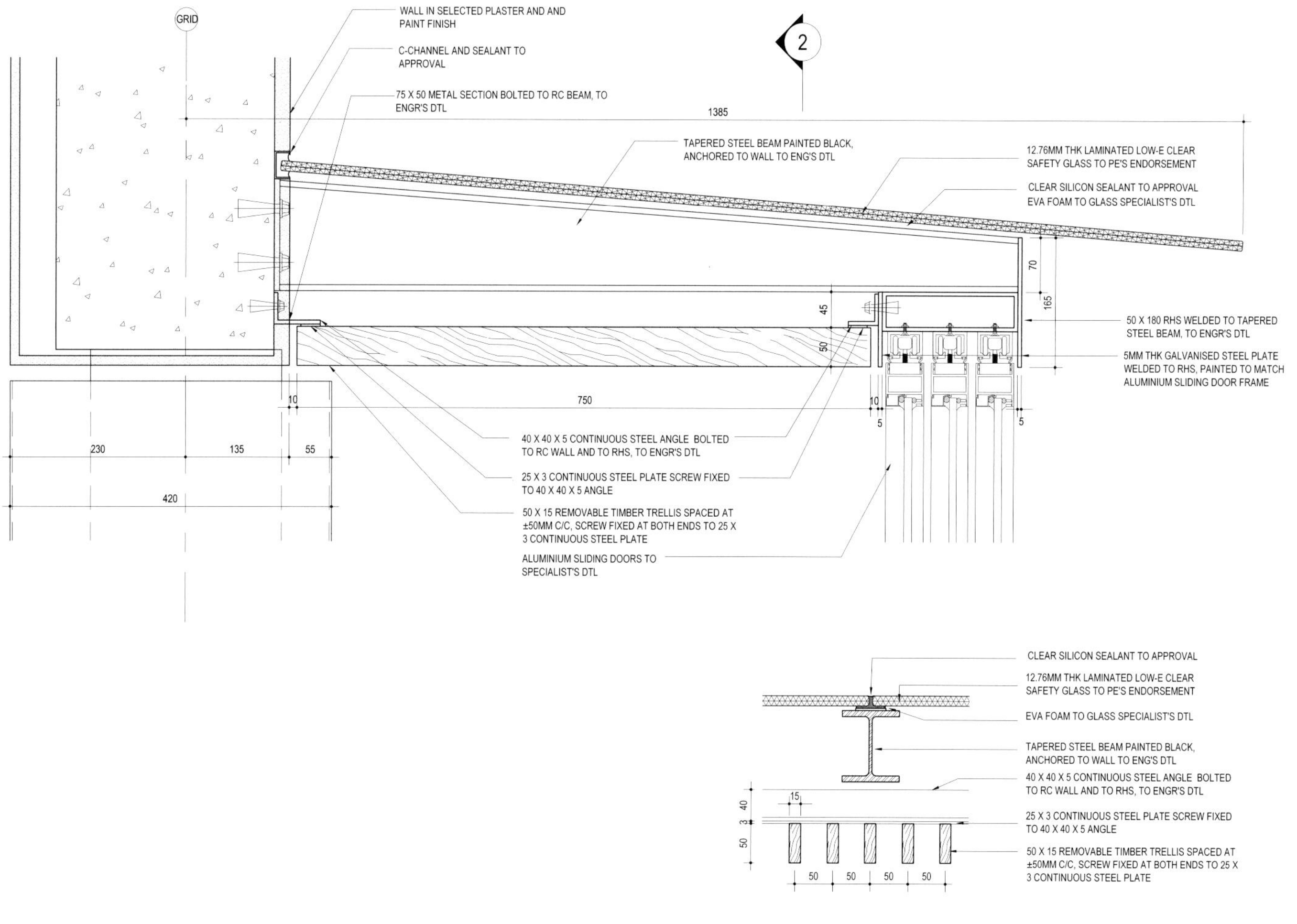

Skylight and Timber Trellis Details Sections

057

Sliding Timber Screen Details

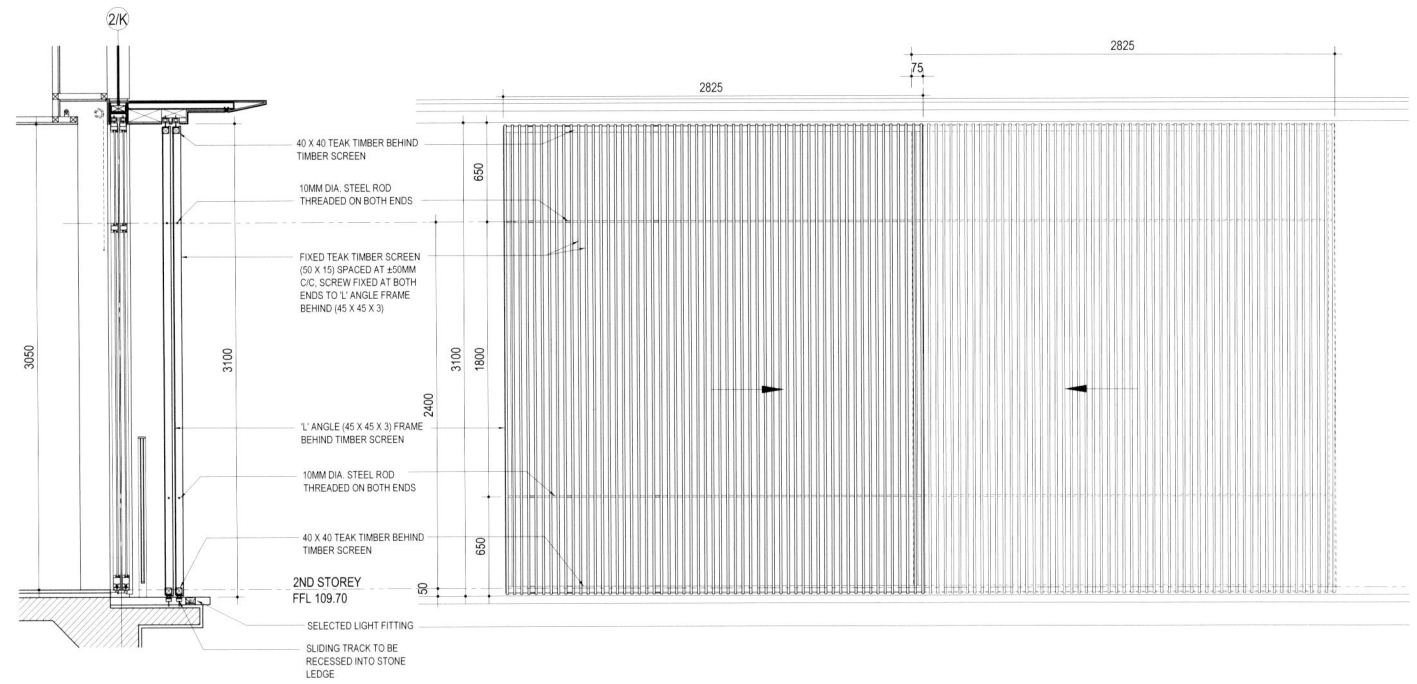

Section   Elevation

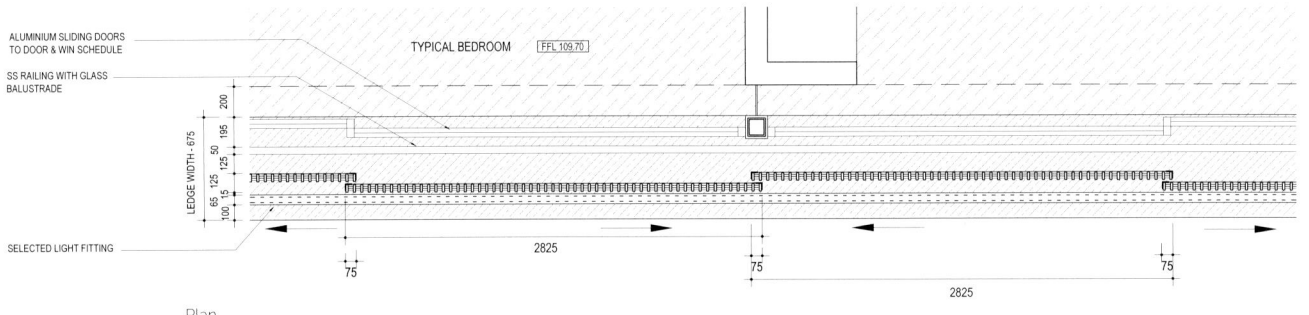

Plan

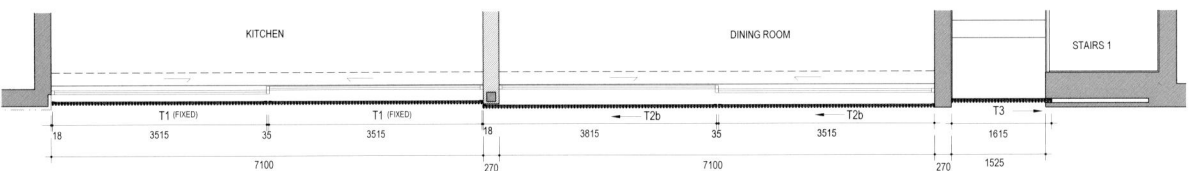

Fully Closed Position

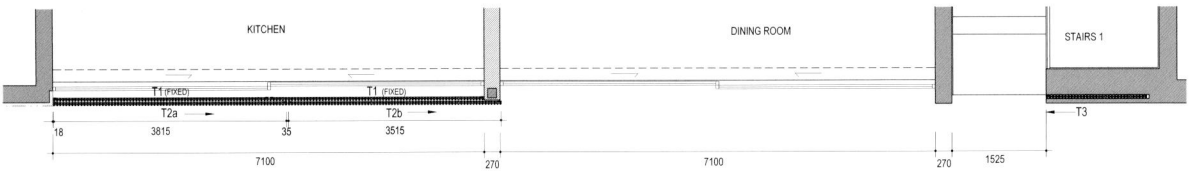

Fully Opened Position

058 | CONSTRUCTION / WORKING DRAWINGS

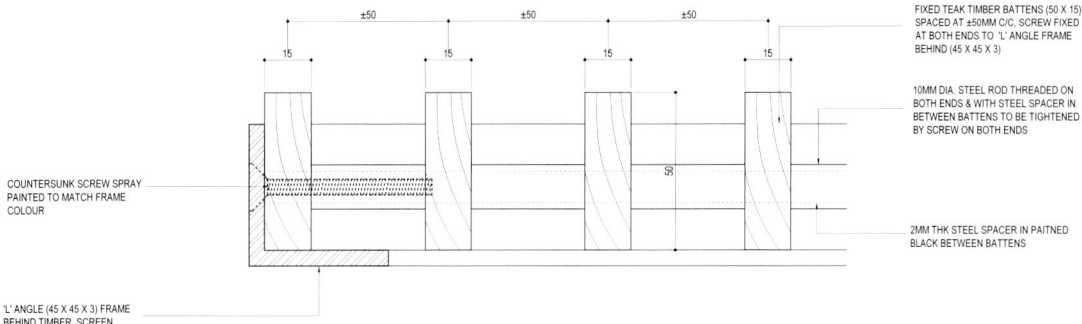

Enlarged Detail Plan

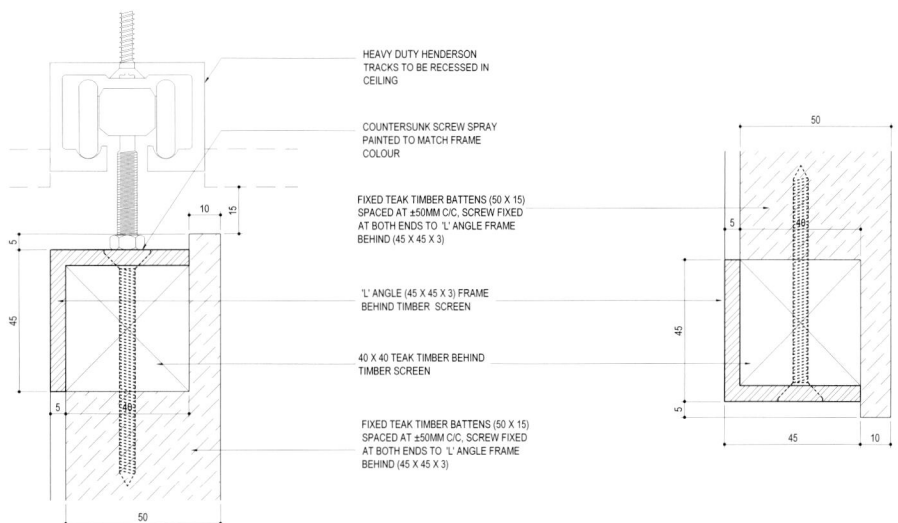

Enlarged Section Details

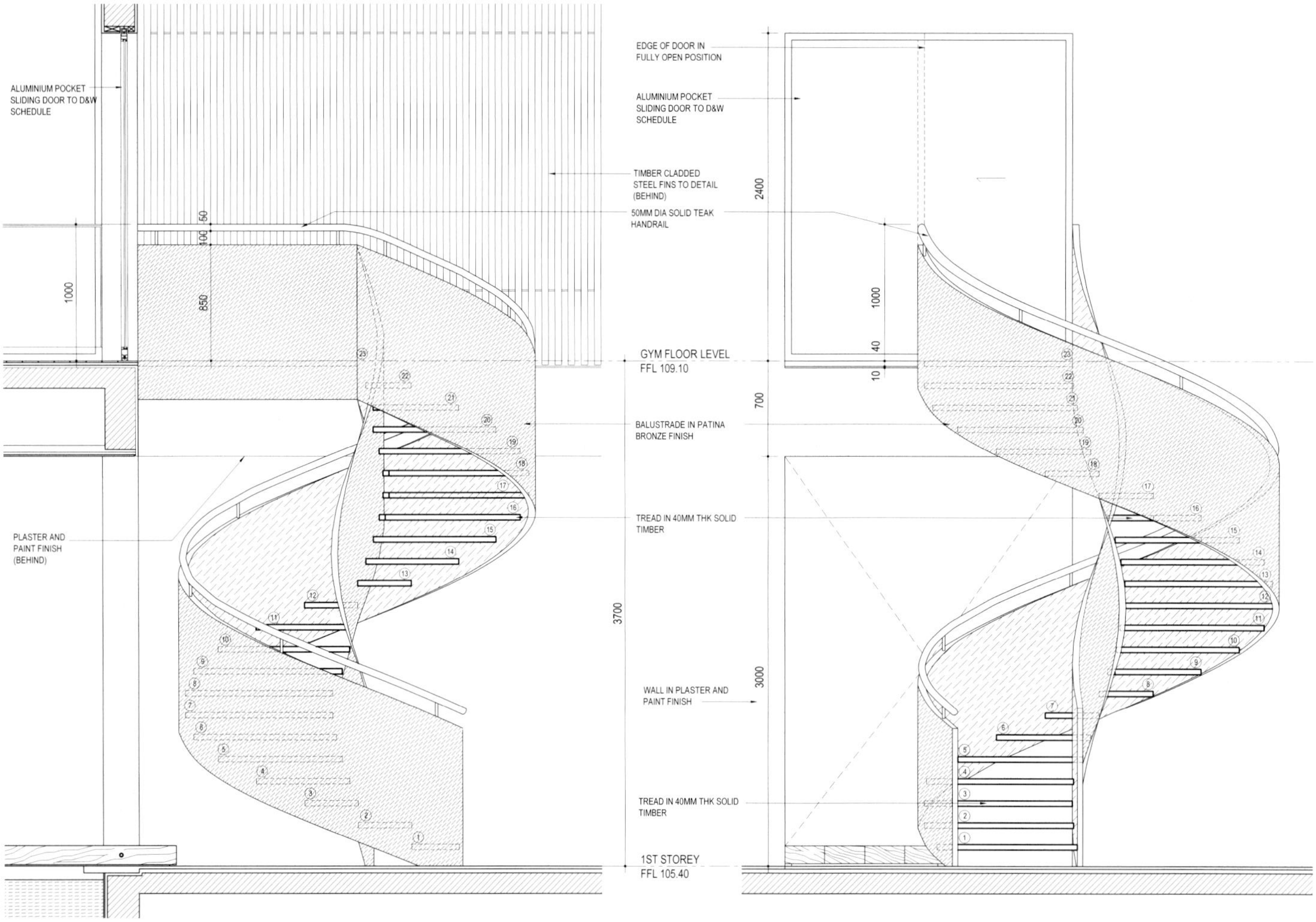

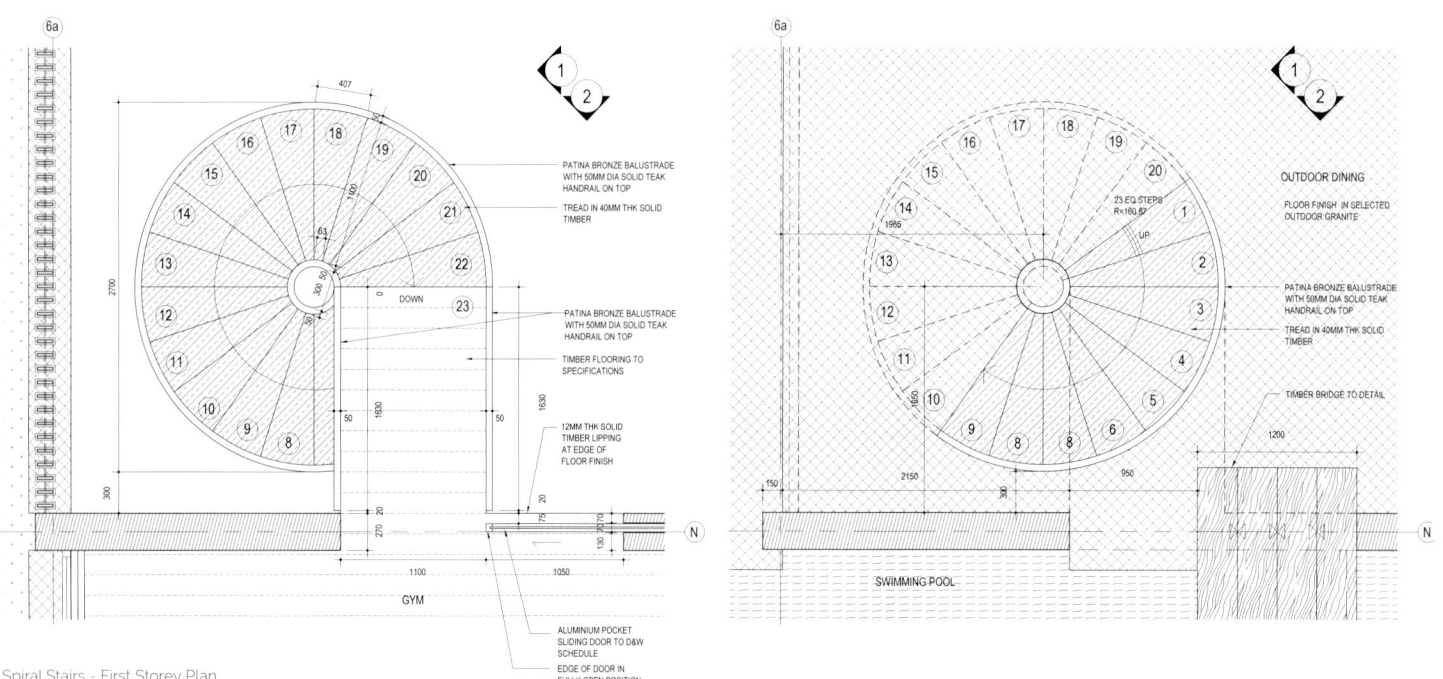

Spiral Stairs - Elevation 1 & 2

Spiral Stairs - First Storey Plan

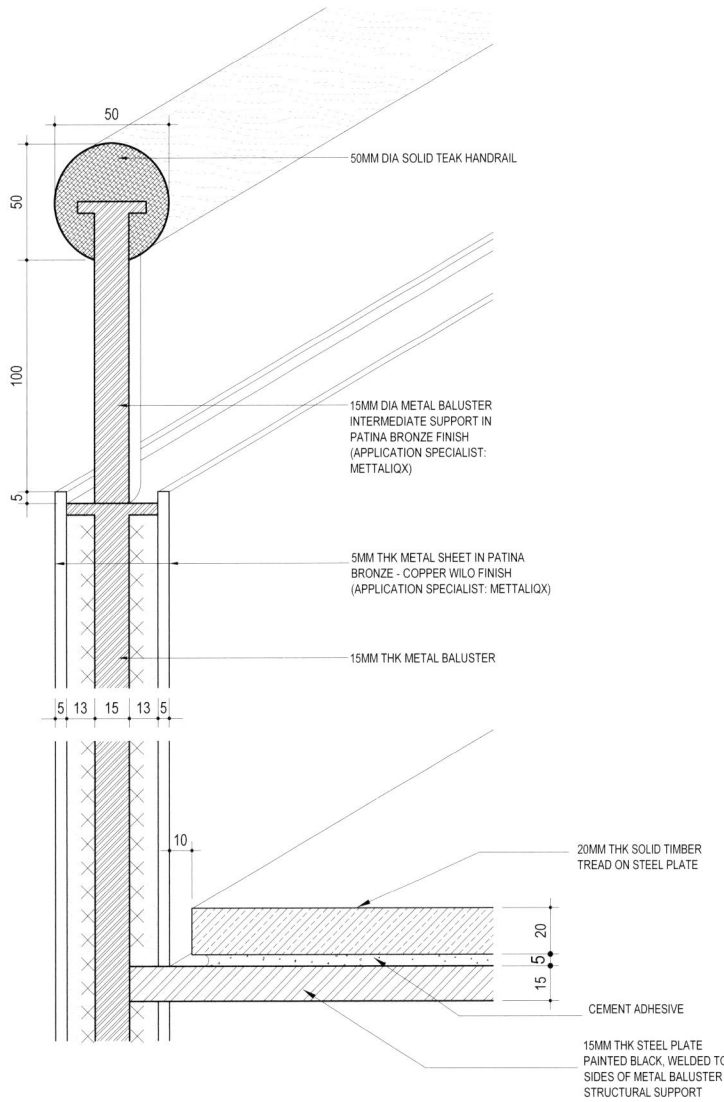

Spiral Stairs - Detail of SS Balustrade

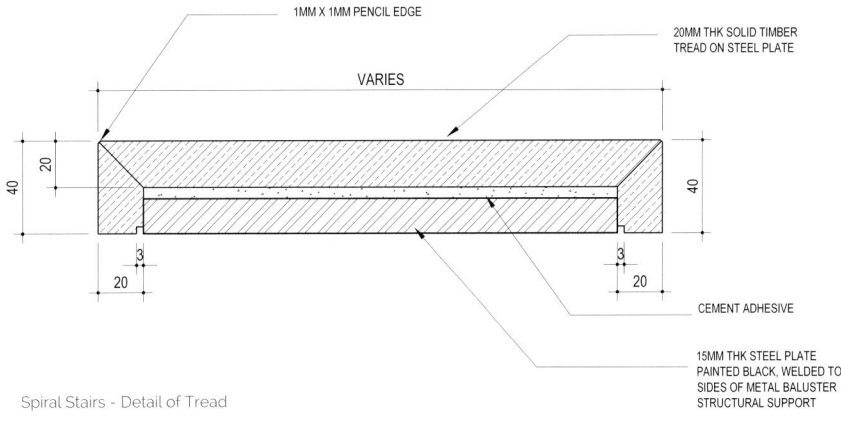

Spiral Stairs - Detail of Tread

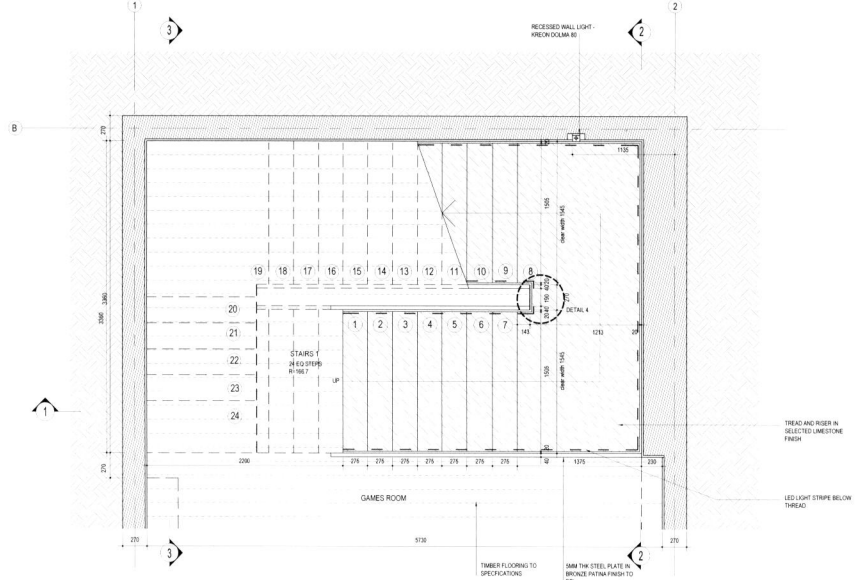

Staircase 1 - Basement Plan

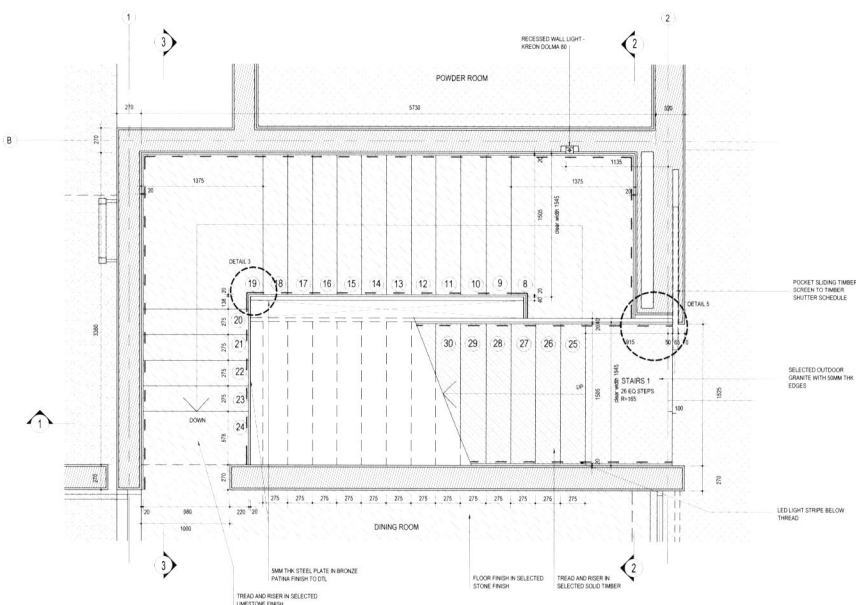

Staircase 1 - First Storey Plan

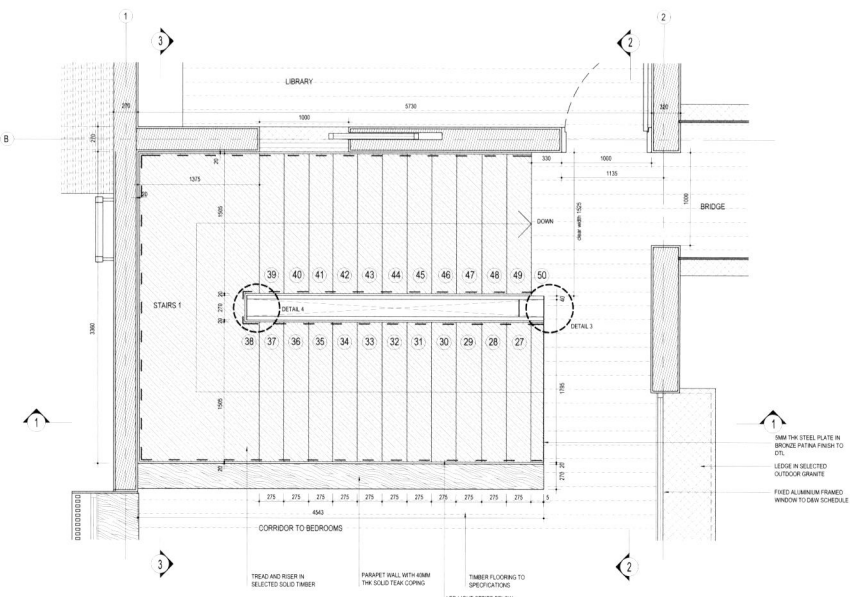

Staircase 1 - Second Storey Plan

062 | CONSTRUCTION / WORKING DRAWINGS

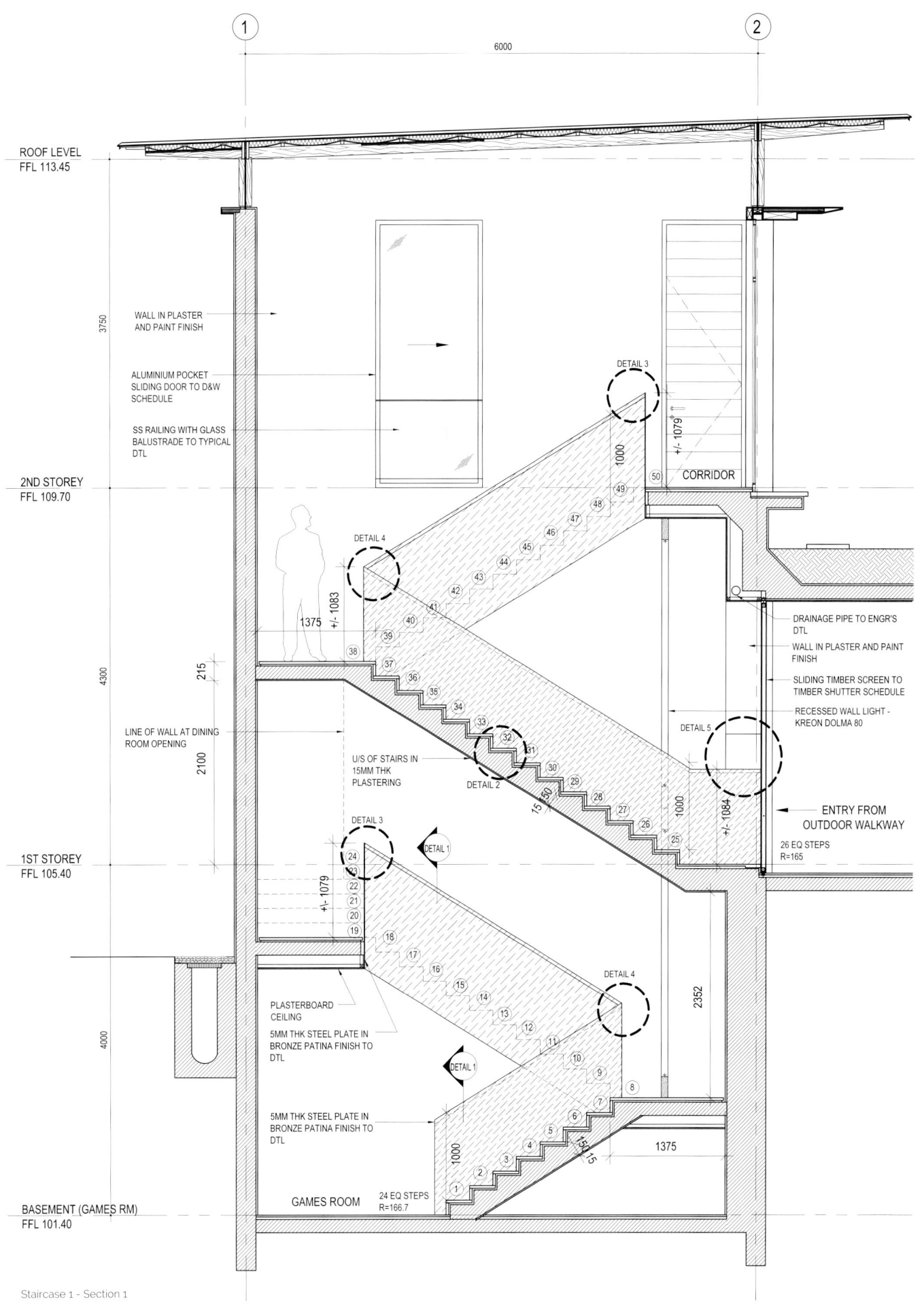

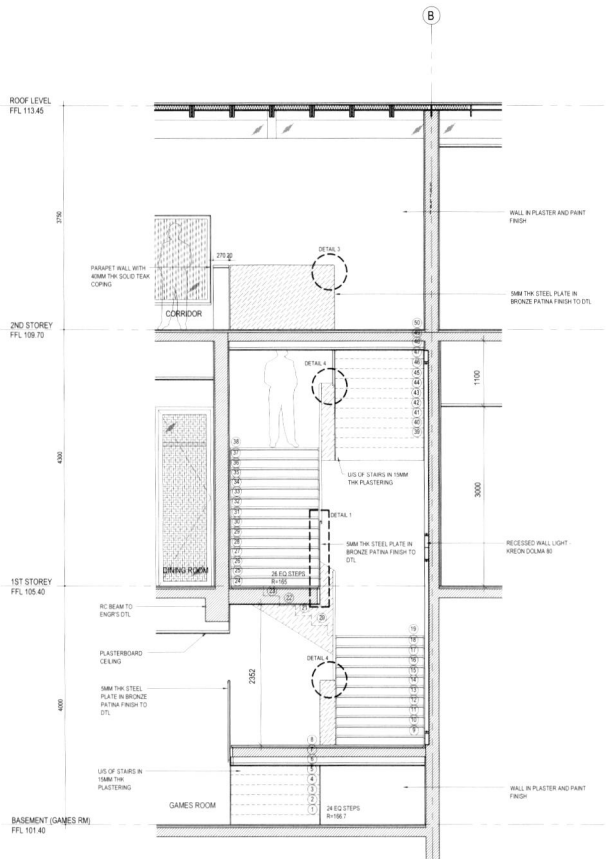

Staircase 1 - Section 2

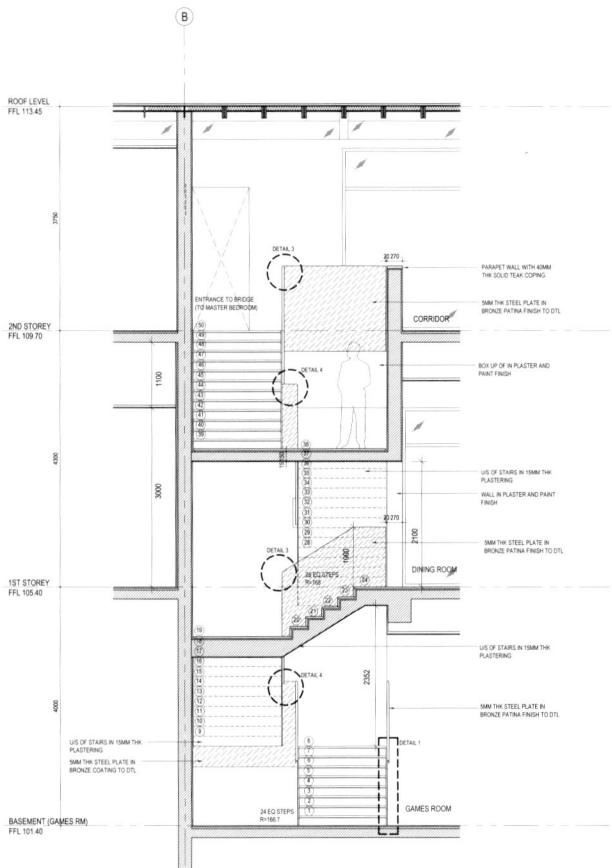

Staircase 1 - Section 2

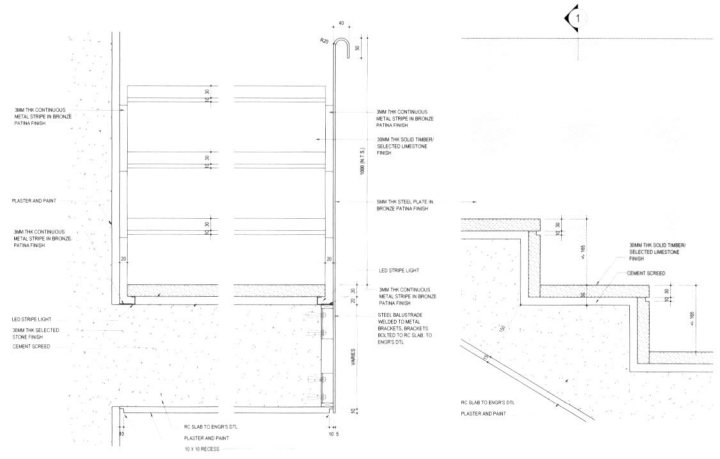

Staircase Detail 1   Staircase Detail 2

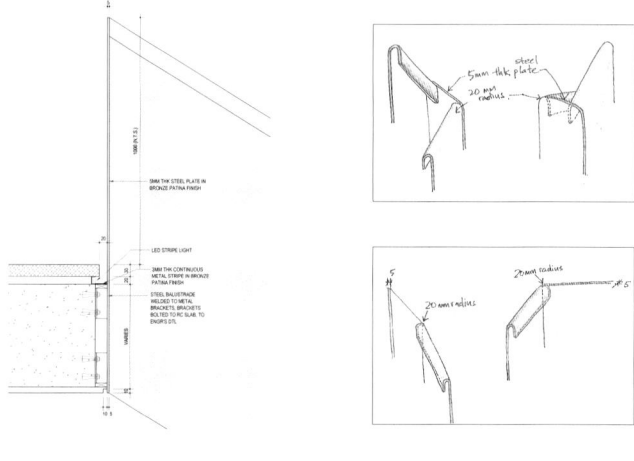

Staircase Detail 3   Staircase Detail 3 & 4 - 3D Sketch N.T.S.

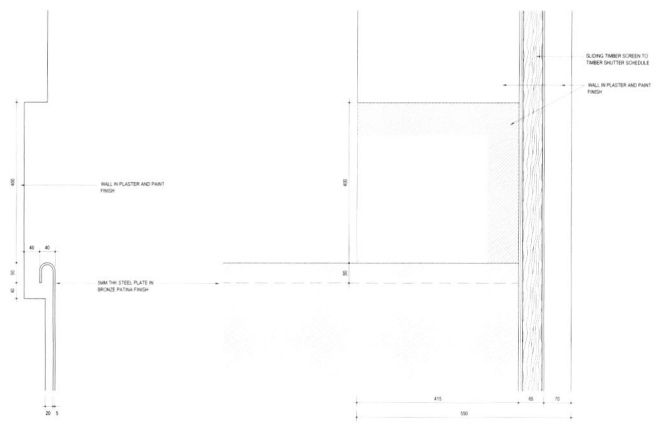

Staircase Detail 5 - Side & Front Elevation

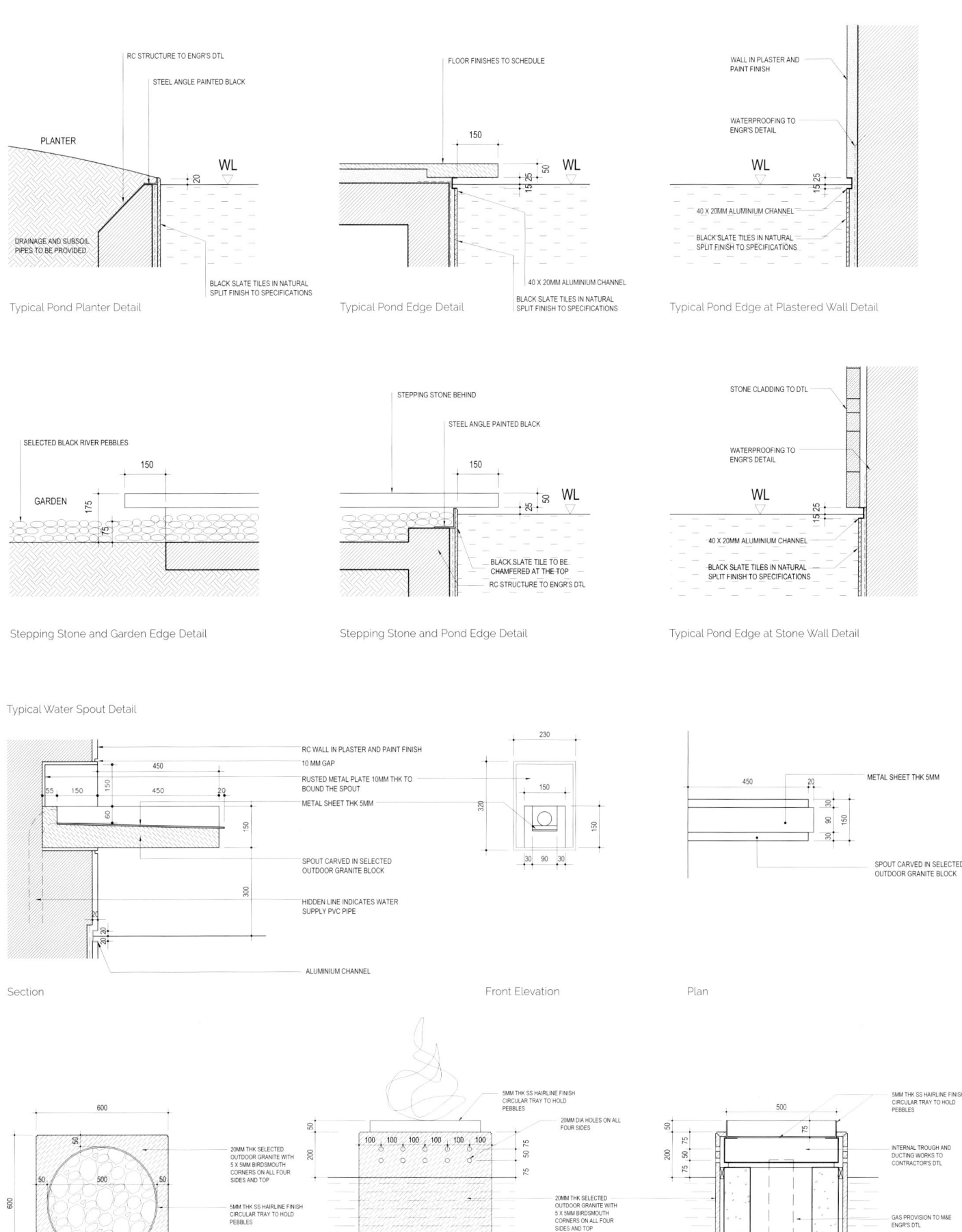

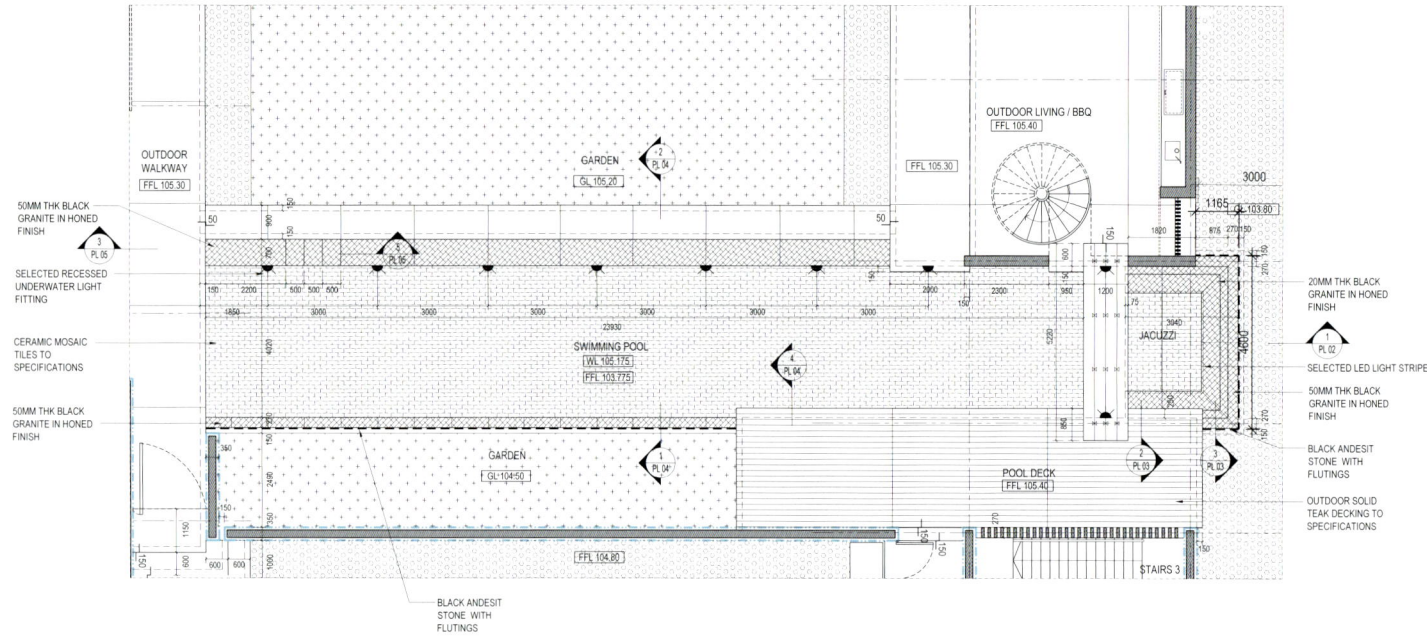

Swimming Pool and Jacuzzi - Key Plan

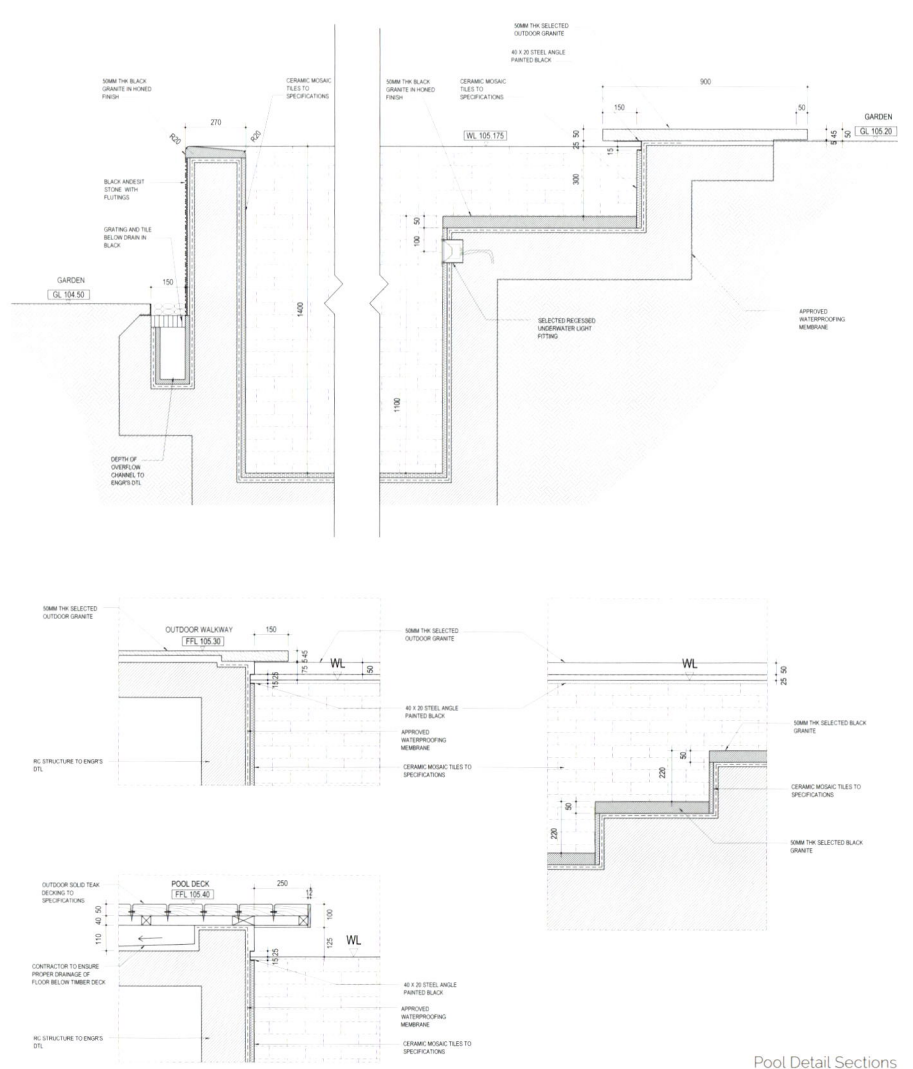

Pool Detail Sections

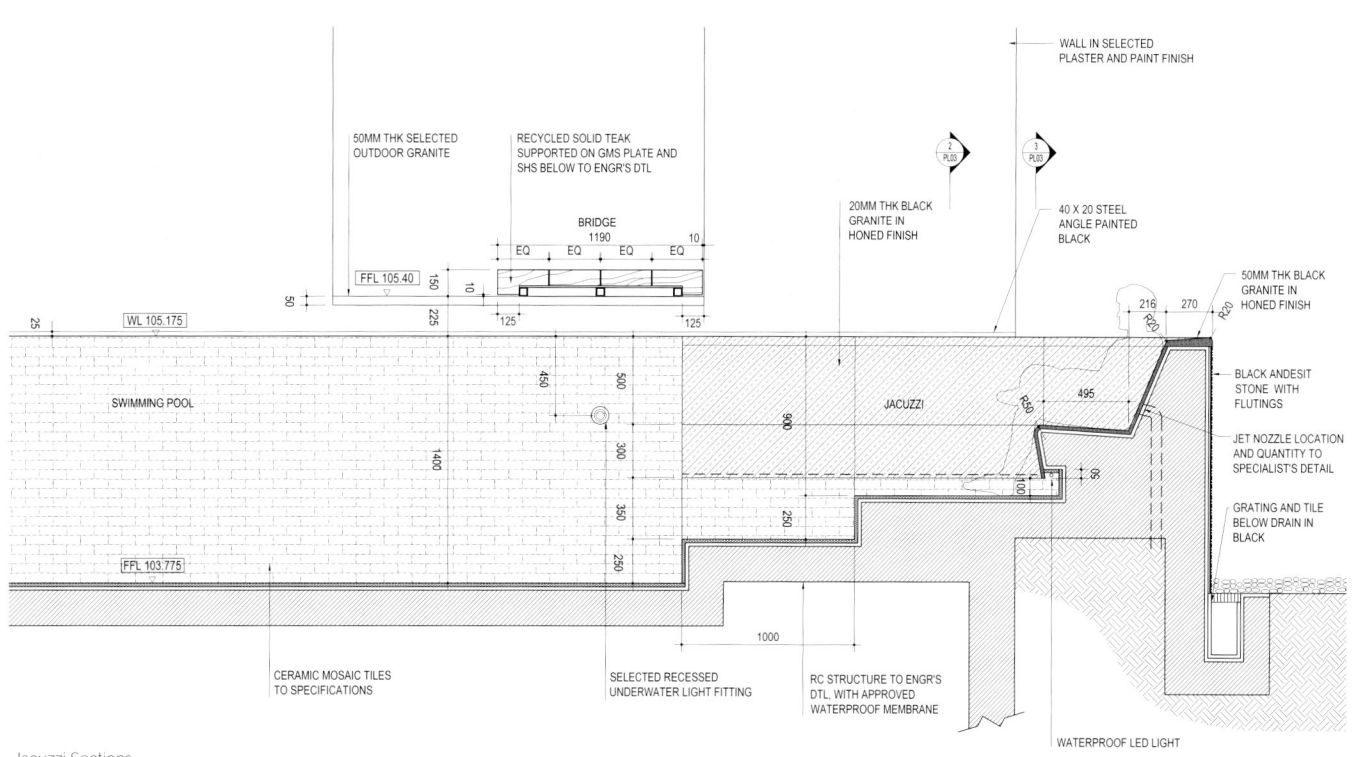

Jacuzzi Sections

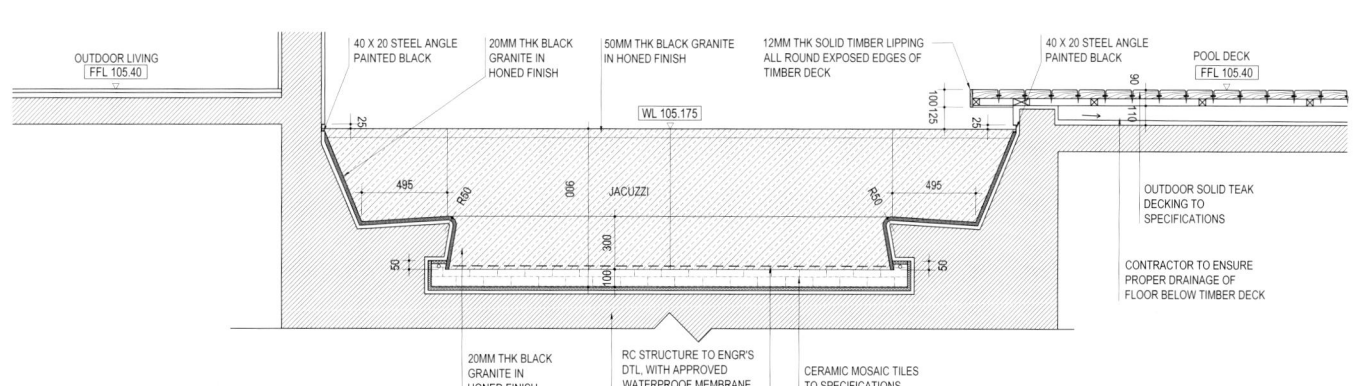

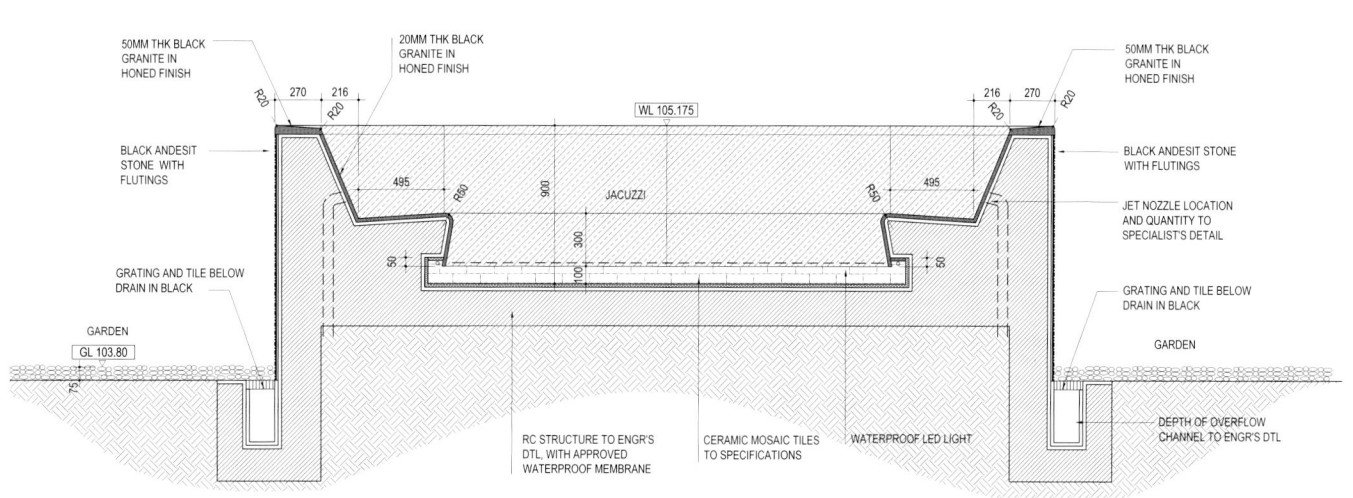

PROCESS

070 | CONSTRUCTION / PROCESS

074 | CONSTRUCTION / PROCESS

081

082 | CONSTRUCTION / PROCESS

084 | CONSTRUCTION / PROCESS

090 | CONSTRUCTION / PROCESS

092 | CONSTRUCTION / PROCESS

THE BUILDING

102 | THE BUILDING

108 | THE BUILDING

109

146 | THE BUILDING

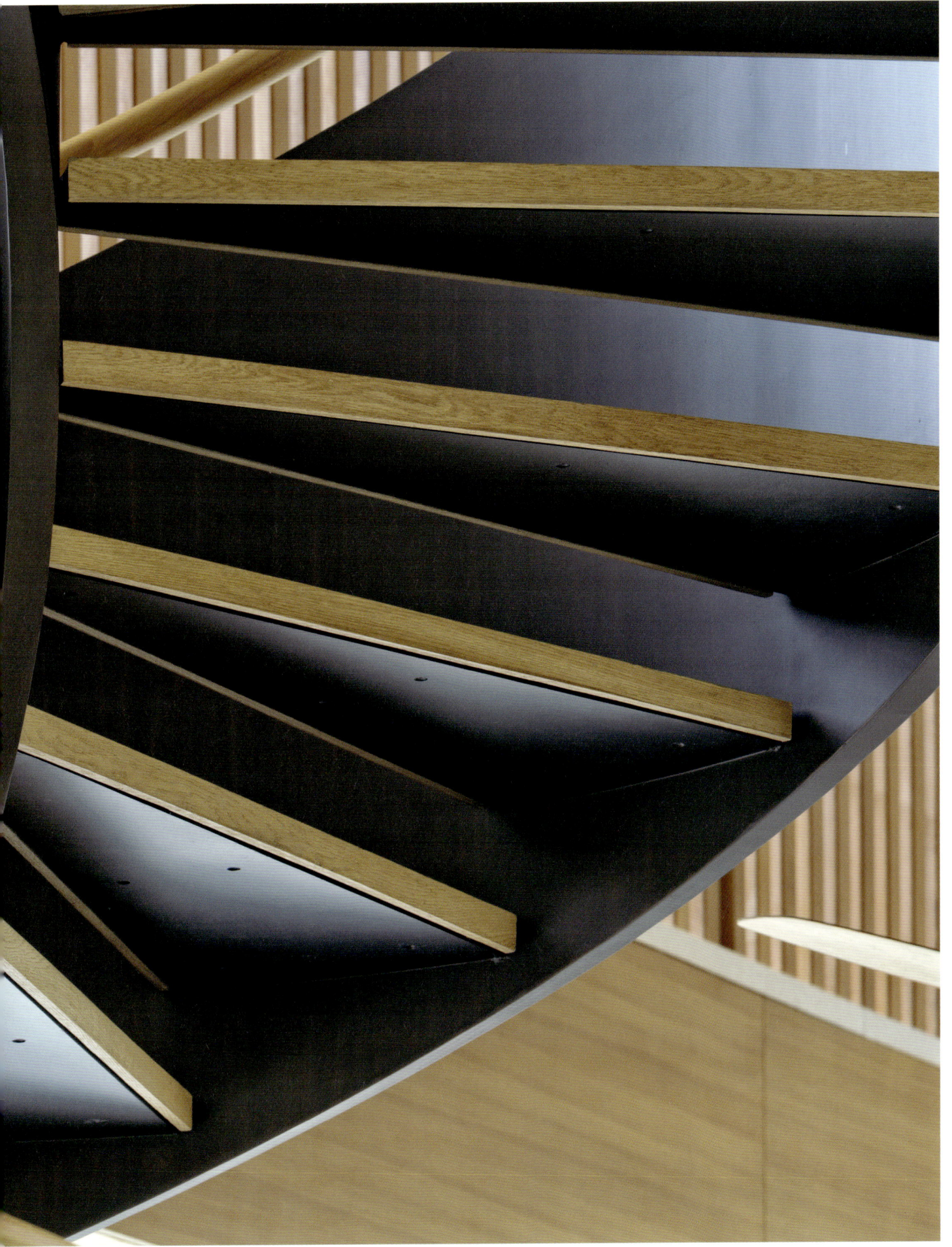

160 | THE BUILDING

165

174 | THE BUILDING

175

EPILOGUE
BY MAX STRANG

Ernesto Bedmar has delivered a masterpiece of 'regional modernism' with the Chancery Lane house. By respecting its specific urban site and honoring the climatic considerations of the tropics, the home is a well-adapted expression of residential architectural design. The courtyard-style arrangement and its modern interpretations of traditional Singaporean designs further reinforce the connection of the house to its unique time and place. The home itself offers immense privacy while simultaneously offering a seamless connection between the interior and exterior spaces. This hard-to-achieve balance of openness and seclusion nurtures the human soul.

Regionalism in architecture is essential to advancing character and culture while reinforcing the magic of a sense-of-place. In academic circles, 'regional modernism' (also referred to as 'critical regionalism') is viewed as an antidote to the sterility of most modern or post-modern architecture. Regional modernism is an approach to design that seeks to mediate between the prevailing universal styles and the honest expressions of a particular locale. In this sense, Bedmar has established himself as a leading proponent and accomplished practitioner of 'regional modernism' and the house at Chancery Lane beautifully demonstrates his mastery. The architecture eschews the placelessness of many modern residences and instead celebrates a uniquely tropical and uniquely Singaporean response. In so doing, the house deftly cuts into the everlasting dance of sun and shade that defines life in the tropics.

From within and without, the architecture reads as a thoughtful composition of space, texture and light. Every surface has been carefully considered as to its individual role in the entire assemblage. Natural woods and stone are contrasted by walls of glass and details of sculpted steel. A rhythm of structure underscores the authenticity of the design and the science behind it all. On the exterior, the purposeful and dramatic sun-shielding elements give the home its identity. The interiors are awash in natural light with escapist views of the surrounding greenery. Each room or space easily blends into the next. This is also a house that bears witness to the romance of the natural world. Invisible breezes filter into the courtyard and give permission to the Frangipani trees to drop their flowers. These specks of color make their way onto the surface of the dark pools below as their ripples reflect in all directions. Deeply shaded terraces are aimed at the meditative views of this calm, private and internalized realm on Chancery Lane.

Intensely tropical and hyper local, the house is assured a respected position along the timeline of 'regional modernism' in Singapore. Well-informed by the culture and architecture that came before it, the home offers a sophisticated vision of how life in the tropics should be lived today and into the future.

MAX STRANG is the Founding Principal of [STRANG]. Through his work and discourse, he has consistently underscored the ongoing relevance and importance of regional modernism to an international audience. Strang is a member of the College of Fellows of the American Institute of Architects and is also a recipient of the Medal of Honor from the Florida Chapter of the AIA, their highest design honor. Strang provides ongoing strategic and creative oversight to the firm and serves as an engaging mentor for its architects, designers and project managers. Additionally, he has led design studios at the University of Miami, Florida International University and the University of Florida. Prior to launching the firm in 2001, Strang worked in the offices of Zaha Hadid and SHoP Architects. The architect that most influenced him, however, was Florida's Gene Leedy, a pioneering member of the Sarasota School of Architecture. Strang was raised in a home designed by Leedy and later interned at his Winter Haven office. He is a graduate of the University of Florida and Columbia University.

APPENDIX

BIOGRAPHY

Ernesto Bedmar was born in Argentina and received a Bachelor of Architecture degree from the University of Architecture and Urban Planning, Córdoba, Argentina, in 1980, receiving the Award for Best Design in his final year. He is a Registered Architect in Argentina and Singapore, as well a Corporate Member of the Singapore Institute of Architects. Ernesto's career began in 1977 when he did practical work at the Miguel Angel Roca Studio in Argentina. In 1980 he became an Associate at Miguel Angel Roca, South Africa, and designed a town planning project for Protea NewTown – South Africa and the Jabulani Administrative Centre in South Africa where he worked with the Architects M.A. Roca and F. Pienaar. In 1982 he was made an Associate at Miguel Angel Roca, Hong Kong, to develop the Tai Long Wan Tourist Resort on Lantau Island, HK. He then joined Palmer & Turner, Hong Kong, as a Consultant Architect in 1983 and was involved in a vast urban project for Macau as a member of the planning group under Architect Alvaro Siza Vieira.

In 1984 he came to Singapore and worked with SAA Partnership until 1986 when he set up his own practice, BEDMaR & SHi Designers Pte Ltd and since then has been a Director/Design Consultant at the company. From 1989 to 2000 Ernesto was a part-time tutor at the School of Architecture at the National University of Singapore and from 1993 to 1995 he was a Member of Design Committee of the Temasek Polytechnic, Singapore, where he also acted as External Examiner for the Bachelor of Arts (Architecture/Hons) program from 2007 to 2010. In early 2009 Ernesto was invited by the Architecture Society at The National University of Singapore to give a guest lecture and in May 2009 he was invited by Raffles University, Singapore, to act as an External Examiner for Design Programmes.

In July 2018 Ernesto Bedmar set up a new establishment 'Ernesto Bedmar Architects Pte Ltd' in association with Ar. Iylia Zakaria and all his current activities are run under the auspices of this company.

He has received several awards including the following listed here in chronological order: 1989 Du Pont Antron Design Award – Honorary Prize – Store Planning Category; 2000 No. 15 Whitehouse Park – Architectural Heritage Awards (URA); 2002 Merit Prize (by Singapore Institute of Architects – Hunter Douglas Design Competition); 2006 3 Houses at Jervois and Trevose 12 – The Chicago Athenaeum International Architecture Award; 2006 Cityscape Architectural Review Awards 2006 Dubai – Winner of Residential Built Award; and 2010 10th SIA Architectural Design Awards for the Recreational Buildings and Individual Houses Categories.

PROJECT CREDITS

Architect
Ernesto Bedmar
for Bedmar & Shi Pte Ltd

Design Team
Ernesto Bedmar
Yap Shan Ming
Tan Chiew Hong
Alvin Jo

Location:
Novena, Singapore

Client:
D. L.

Project Year:
2014

Completion:
2017

Land Area:
1862.7 m²

Built Area:
1247.9 m²

Photography:
Claudio Manzoni
Albert Lim

General Contractor:
Huat Builders Pte Ltd

Structural Engineering:
Tham & Wong LLP

M&E Engineering:
PTA Consultants Pte Ltd

Quantity Surveyor:
Ian Chng Consultants Pte Ltd

Interior Design:
Bedmar & Shi Pte Ltd
ANP Interior Architecture

Landscape Design:
Bedmar & Shi Pte Ltd

Landscape Contractor:
Kok Keong Landscape Pte Ltd

Lighting:
Lightcraft Pte Ltd

Furnishing:
Christian Liaigre

Kitchen:
Arclinea Singapore Pte Ltd

PHOTOGRAPHY CAPTIONS

Swimming pool and garden view.
Photograph by Claudio Manzoni.

Detail of spiral stairs. View from gym level.
Photograph by Claudio Manzoni.

Detail of the framings at the front of the house.
Photograph by Claudio Manzoni.

Detail of the end of the swimming pool (jacuzzi area). 50mm black granite in honed finish and black andesit stone with flutings.
Photograph by Claudio Manzoni.

Pond.
Photograph by Claudio Manzoni.

Garden, south view.
Photograph by Albert Lim.

Construction process.
Site before excavation.
Photograph by Ernesto Bedmar Architects.

Construction process.
Foundation construction.
Photograph by Ernesto Bedmar Architects.

Construction process.
Photograph by Ernesto Bedmar Architects.

Construction process.
Photograph by Ernesto Bedmar Architects.

Construction process.
Photograph by Ernesto Bedmar Architects.

Construction process.
Excavation.
Photograph by Ernesto Bedmar Architects.

Construction process.
Photograph by Ernesto Bedmar Architects.

Construction process.
Photograph by Ernesto Bedmar Architects.

Construction process.
Photograph by Ernesto Bedmar Architects.

Construction process. Wall construction.
Photograph by Ernesto Bedmar Architects.

Construction process.
Photograph by Ernesto Bedmar Architects.

Construction process.
Photograph by Ernesto Bedmar Architects.

Construction process.
Photograph by Ernesto Bedmar Architects.

Construction process.
Photograph by Ernesto Bedmar Architects.

Construction process.
Photograph by Ernesto Bedmar Architects.

Construction process.
Pond construction.
Photograph by Ernesto Bedmar Architects.

Construction process.
Pond construction.
Photograph by Ernesto Bedmar Architects.

Construction process.
Photograph by Ernesto Bedmar Architects.

Construction process.
Photograph by Ernesto Bedmar Architects.

Construction process.
Photograph by Ernesto Bedmar Architects.

Construction process.
Photograph by Ernesto Bedmar Architects.

Construction process.
Photograph by Ernesto Bedmar Architects.

Construction process.
Photograph by Ernesto Bedmar Architects.

Construction process.
Photograph by Ernesto Bedmar Architects.

Construction process.
Photograph by Ernesto Bedmar Architects.

Construction process.
Photograph by Ernesto Bedmar Architects.

Construction process.
Photograph by Ernesto Bedmar Architects.

Construction process.
Photograph by Ernesto Bedmar Architects.

Construction process.
Pond construction.
Photograph by Ernesto Bedmar Architects.

Construction process.
Stair construction.
Photograph by Ernesto Bedmar Architects.

Construction process.
Photograph by Ernesto Bedmar Architects.

Construction process.
Photograph by Ernesto Bedmar Architects.

Construction process.
Photograph by Ernesto Bedmar Architects.

Construction process.
Photograph by Ernesto Bedmar Architects.

Construction process.
Wood wall cladding detail.
Photograph by Ernesto Bedmar Architects.

Construction process.
Stone wall cladding detail.
Photograph by Ernesto Bedmar Architects.

Construction process.
Photograph by Ernesto Bedmar Architects.

Construction process.
Photograph by Ernesto Bedmar Architects.

Construction process.
Swimming pool construction.
Photograph by Ernesto Bedmar Architects.

Construction process.
Swimming pool and driveway wall construction.
Photograph by Ernesto Bedmar Architects.

Construction process.
Swimming pool construction.
Photograph by Ernesto Bedmar Architects.

Construction process.
Swimming pool construction.
Photograph by Ernesto Bedmar Architects.

Construction process.
Photograph by Ernesto Bedmar Architects.

Construction process.
Planter construction detail.
Photograph by Ernesto Bedmar Architects.

Construction process.
Wood roof detail.
Photograph by Ernesto Bedmar Architects.

Construction process.
Conditioning detail.
Photograph by Ernesto Bedmar Architects.

Construction process.
Photograph by Ernesto Bedmar Architects.

Construction process.
Photograph by Ernesto Bedmar Architects.

Construction process.
Photograph by Ernesto Bedmar Architects.

Construction process.
Photograph by Ernesto Bedmar Architects.

Construction process.
Photograph by Ernesto Bedmar Architects.

Construction process.
Photograph by Ernesto Bedmar Architects.

Construction process.
Photograph by Ernesto Bedmar Architects.

Construction process.
Alumnium roof detail.
Photograph by Ernesto Bedmar Architects.

Construction process.
Photograph by Ernesto Bedmar Architects.

Construction process.
Timber bridge construction.
Photograph by Ernesto Bedmar Architects.

Construction process.
Timber bridge construction.
Photograph by Ernesto Bedmar Architects.

Construction process.
Photograph by Ernesto Bedmar Architects.

Construction process.
Photograph by Ernesto Bedmar Architects.

Construction process.
Swimming pool, jacuzzi and pool deck construction.
Photograph by Ernesto Bedmar Architects.

Construction process.
Wall construction, lighting installation.
Photograph by Ernesto Bedmar Architects.

Construction process.
Pond area.
Photograph by Ernesto Bedmar Architects.

Construction process.
Photograph by Ernesto Bedmar Architects.

Construction process.
Pond construction.
Photograph by Ernesto Bedmar Architects.

Construction process.
Perimeter wall, sliding entry door detail.
Photograph by Ernesto Bedmar Architects.

Construction process.
Spiral stair construction.
Photograph by Ernesto Bedmar Architects.

Construction process.
Spiral stair construction. Tread in 40mm solid timber.
Photograph by Ernesto Bedmar Architects.

Construction process.
Spiral stair construction.
Photograph by Ernesto Bedmar Architects.

Construction process.
Stair construction. 3mm continuous metal stripe in bronze patina finish.
Photograph by Ernesto Bedmar Architects.

Construction process.
Stair construction.
Photograph by Ernesto Bedmar Architects.

Construction process.
Stair construction. Cement screed.
Photograph by Ernesto Bedmar Architects.

Construction process.
Photograph by Ernesto Bedmar Architects.

Construction process.
Photograph by Ernesto Bedmar Architects.

Construction process.
Photograph by Ernesto Bedmar Architects.

Construction process.
Garden surface preparation for sod.
Photograph by Ernesto Bedmar Architects.

Construction process.
Photograph by Ernesto Bedmar Architects.

Construction process.
Stair construction. Bronze patina balustrade with 50mm dia solid teak handrail on top.
Photograph by Ernesto Bedmar Architects.

Construction process.
Living room, reinforced concrete column with metal cladding, mirror pocket sliding door and fixed panel.
Photograph by Ernesto Bedmar Architects.

Construction process.
Aluminium pocket sliding door to d&w schedule. Wall in plaster and paint finish.
Photograph by Ernesto Bedmar Architects.

Construction process.
Garden and corridor detail.
Photograph by Ernesto Bedmar Architects.

Construction process.
Photograph by Ernesto Bedmar Architects.

Construction process.
Photograph by Ernesto Bedmar Architects.

Building street view.
Photograph by Caludio Manzoni.

Building, full front exterior view.
Photograph by Caludio Manzoni.

Entry with wooden gate opened.
Photograph by Caludio Manzoni.

Entry, entry drop-off and car porch.
Photograph by Albert Lim.

Exterior perimeter stone wall.
Photograph by Caludio Manzoni.

Entry and car porch, view from planter.
Photograph by Caludio Manzoni.

Detail of entry planter corner.
Photograph by Caludio Manzoni.

Entry drop-off, planter and second floor bedroom.
Photograph by Caludio Manzoni.

Swimming pool and garden view.
Photograph by Caludio Manzoni.

Walkway view of outdoor living/barbecue and pond.
Photograph by Albert Lim.

Distant view of living and family rooms. Wood ceiling.
Photograph by Albert Lim.

Family room view from outdoor living/barbecue, firepit.
Photograph by Albert Lim.

Living room, reinforced concrete column with metal cladding.
Photograph by Caludio Manzoni.

Living room, with pond view.
Photograph by Caludio Manzoni.

Family room with TV console. Steel column in front of mirror with metal cladding in bronze finish, with built-in column light fixture.
Photograph by Caludio Manzoni.

Family room with a view towards the pond.
Photograph by Caludio Manzoni.

Living room.
Photograph by Caludio Manzoni.

Dining room, view towards the garden.
Photograph by Caludio Manzoni.

Dining room and sliding timber screens.
Photograph by Caludio Manzoni.

Outside view of living room corner.
Photograph by Caludio Manzoni.

Living room view from pond. Pedestal for pots in reinforced concrete with black slate cladding and 50mm granite ledge.
Photograph by Caludio Manzoni.

Corner detail at pond.
Photograph by Caludio Manzoni.

Living room view from pond. Glass roof with timber trellis. Aluminum frame sliding/fixed glass doors.
Photograph by Caludio Manzoni.

Pond between family room and outdoor living room/barbecue.
Photograph by Caludio Manzoni.

First storey bathroom with pond view. Shower detail.
Photograph by Claudio Manzoni.

First storey bathroom.
Photograph by Claudio Manzoni.

First storey bathroom.
Photograph by Claudio Manzoni.

Stairs with 1.5mm steel plate in bronze patina finish.
Photograph by Claudio Manzoni.

Parapet wall with 40mm solid teak coping.
Photograph by Claudio Manzoni.

Entrance to bridge (to master bedroom).
Photograph by Claudio Manzoni.

Handrail, 5mm steel plate, 20mm radius.
Photograph by Claudio Manzoni.

3mm continuous metal stripe in bronze patina finish. Wall in plaster and paint finish.
Photograph by Claudio Manzoni.

5mm steel plate in bronze patina finish.
Photograph by Claudio Manzoni.

Led stripe light with 5mm steel plate in bronze patina finish. Steel balustrade welded to metal brackets. Brackets bolted to reinforced concrete slab.
Photograph by Claudio Manzoni.

Bridge, view from library/study. Steel bridge.
Photograph by Claudio Manzoni.

Bridge to master bedroom. Laminated low-e clear tempered frameless fixed glass to pe's endorsement.
Photograph by Claudio Manzoni.

Master bedroom, view to master bathroom. Sliding timber screens. Stainless steel railing with glass balustrade. Aluminium framed sliding doors.
Photograph by Claudio Manzoni.

Master bedroom, view to bridge. Plasterboard ceiling. Wall in plaster and paint finish.
Photograph by Claudio Manzoni.

Master dresser.
Photograph by Claudio Manzoni.

Master bathroom. Pocket timber sliding doors.
Photograph by Claudio Manzoni.

Master bath.
Photograph by Claudio Manzoni.

Corner detail.
Photograph by Claudio Manzoni.

Corridor, bedroom 1. 120 x 120 shs with 15mm thick solid teak cladding all round. Fixed timber screen with alum frame glass sliding windows behind.
Photograph by Claudio Manzoni.

Bedroom 1. Sliding timber screens.
Photograph by Claudio Manzoni.

Upper floor corridor.
Photograph by Claudio Manzoni.

Upper floor corridor. Sliding timber screens. SS railing with glass balustrade. Aluminium framed sliding doors.
Photograph by Claudio Manzoni.

Master bedroom's aluminium roof detail.
Photograph by Claudio Manzoni.

Sliding timber screens and planter.
Photograph by Claudio Manzoni.

Sliding timber screens detail.
Photograph by Claudio Manzoni.

Sliding timber screens, opened. Stainless steel railing with glass balustrade. Aluminium framed sliding doors. Proprietary metal trellis.
Photograph by Claudio Manzoni.

Aluminium roof detail.
Photograph by Claudio Manzoni.

Garden, view from bedroom 3.
Photograph by Claudio Manzoni.

Swimming pool, view from bedroom 3.
Photograph by Albert Lim.

Planter and sliding timber screens.
Photograph by Albert Lim.

Swimming pool, view from bedroom 2.
Photograph by Claudio Manzoni.

Garden, view from bedroom 1.
Photograph by Albert Lim.

 Swimming pool and pool deck. Photograph by Albert Lim.

 Garden view from master dresser. Photograph by Albert Lim.

 Timber bridge detail. Photograph by Albert Lim.

 Swimming pool and pool deck. Photograph by Albert Lim.

 Oudoor living/barbecue, spiral stairs. Timber cladded steel fins (upstairs). Photograph by Claudio Manzoni.

 Spiral stairs detail. Tread in 40mm solid timber. Photograph by Claudio Manzoni.

 Balustrade in patina bronze finish. Photograph by Claudio Manzoni.

 Oudoor living/barbecue, spiral stairs. Photograph by Claudio Manzoni.

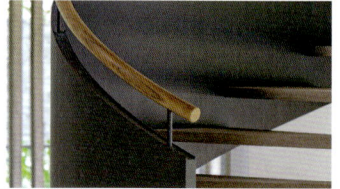 50mm dia solid teak handrail.
15mm dia metal baluster intermediate support in patina bronze finish.
5mm metal sheet in patina bronze - copper wilo finish.
Photograph by Claudio Manzoni.

 Timber screen. Photograph by Claudio Manzoni.

 Timber bridge above pool with steel support below. Photograph by Claudio Manzoni.

 Jacuzzi. 20mm black granite in honed finish. Black andesit stone with flutings. Photograph by Claudio Manzoni.

 Swimming pool deck. Outdoor solid teak decking and timber bridge. Jacuzzi area. Photograph by Claudio Manzoni.

 Ceramic mosaic tiles at pool. Photograph by Claudio Manzoni.

 Swiming pool and deck detail. Outdoor solid teak decking. 50mm selected outdoor granite. Photograph by Claudio Manzoni.

 Ceramic mosaic tiles at pool. Photograph by Claudio Manzoni.

Ceramic mosaic tiles at pool.
Photograph by Claudio Manzoni.

Outdoor solid teak decking and timber bridge.
Photograph by Claudio Manzoni.

Ceramic mosaic tiles at pool.
Photograph by Claudio Manzoni.

Garden view from jacuzzi area.
Photograph by Claudio Manzoni.

Evening view of living room.
Photograph by Claudio Manzoni.

Sliding timber screen and planter detail. Night view.
Photograph by Claudio Manzoni.

Window detail. Night view.
Photograph by Claudio Manzoni.

Kitchen view from swimming pool. Night view.
Photograph by Claudio Manzoni.

Entrance corridor. Night view.
Photograph by Albert Lim.

Swimming pool and pool deck. Night view.
Photograph by Albert Lim.

Outdoor living/barbecue. Night view.
Photograph by Claudio Manzoni.

Living room and pond night view.
Photograph by Claudio Manzoni.

Outdoor living/barbecue and spiral stair. Night view.
Photograph by Claudio Manzoni.

Garden night view.
Photograph by Claudio Manzoni.

Wood wall detail.
Photograph by Claudio Manzoni.

Swimming pool and garden view.
Photograph by Albert Lim.

BOOK CREDITS

Text Editing by Kit Maude
Book Layout by Lucía B. Bauzá
Art Director: Oscar Riera Ojeda

OSCAR RIERA OJEDA
PUBLISHERS

Copyright © 2020 by Oscar Riera Ojeda Publishers Limited
ISBN 978-1-946226-09-9
Published by Oscar Riera Ojeda Publishers Limited
Printed in China

Oscar Riera Ojeda Publishers Limited
Unit 1003-04, 10/F.,
Shanghai Industrial Investment Building,
48-62 Hennessy Road, Wanchai, Hong Kong
T: +852-3920-9300

Production Offices | China
Suit 19, Shenyun Road,
Nanshan District, Shenzhen 518055
T: +1-484-502-5400

www.oropublishers.com | www.oscarrieraojeda.com
oscar@oscarrieraojeda.com

All rights reserved. No part of this book may be reproduced, stored in a retrieval system, or transmitted in any form or by any means, including electronic, mechanical, photocopying of microfilming, recording, or otherwise (except that copying permitted by Sections 107 and 108 of the U.S. Copyright Law and except by reviewers for the public press) without written permission from the publisher.